POWER, PASSION
&PRAYER

POWER, PASSION
& PRAYER

CHARLES G. FINNEY

Bridge-Logos
Newberry, FL 32669 USA

Bridge-Logos

Newberry, FL 32669 USA

Power, Passion and Prayer
by Charles G. Finney
Rewritten and Updated by Robert A. Engelhardt

TABLE OF CONTENTS

BIOGRAPHY OF

CHARLES GRANDISON FINNEY

1792 - 1875

The man whom many believe was the greatest revivalists that ever lived, a man through whom the convicting power of the Holy Spirit flowed not like a river but like a flood, was born in Warren, Litchfield County, Connecticut, on August 29, 1792, to Sylvester and Rebecca Finney. When he was about two years old, his parents moved to Oneida County, New York, which at that time was mainly a wilderness. Because of the sparse population there were few churches in the area and few religious books available.

Most of the settlers in the area were from New England, and as was their previous custom they immediately established common schools, which were elementary public schools. There was, however, little intelligent preaching of the Gospel in the schools. Finney attended the common school summer and winter until he was 15 or 16 years old; and he advanced so far that he became capable of conducting a common school himself, which was normal practice in those days.

Neither of Finney's parents professed any religious belief, and few of his neighbors were religious people. He seldom heard a sermon, except for an occasional one from some traveling minister, or as he put it, "some miserable putting forth of an ignorant preacher would sometimes be found in that country." The ignorance of the preachers was often so great that when the people left the meetings they spent a considerable time laughing at the strange mistakes that had been made and the absurdities that had been put forth as the Gospel.

Eventually a meeting house was erected near his parent's house and a minister obtained for it, but his parents moved again to the wilderness along the southern shore of Lake Ontario, just south of Sacketts Harbor. Finney lived there for several years but had no better religious training than he had in Oneida County.

When he was about 20 years old, he returned to Connecticut to live with an uncle, and from there went to New Jersey, near New York City, and started teaching. Although Finney only had a common school education, he taught and studied as well as he could. Twice he returned to New England and attended a high school for a season. While attending high school he thought about going to Yale College, but his teacher advised against it. He said that Finney could easily accomplish the entire curriculum in two years, but he would have to spend four years to graduate. He was so persuasive that Finney did not pursue his formal education any further. Later he did acquire some knowledge of Latin, Greek, and Hebrew, but never enough to consider himself capable of independently criticizing the English translation of the Bible.

In 1818, Finney was thinking of moving south, but when he informed his parents, whom he hadn't seen in four years, they immediately traveled to where he was and prevailed upon him to go home with them to Jefferson County, New York. Not long after, he started working as a student in the law office of Squire Wright, in the town of Adams in Jefferson County.

Up to this time Finney had never received any religious training, except while he was attending high school in New England. The aged minister at the church he attended, although an excellent man and well loved by his people, read his sermons in such a way that they barely caught Finney's attention. Finney said,

> "To give some idea of his preaching, let me say that his manuscript sermons were just large enough to put into a small Bible. I sat in the gallery, and observed that he placed his manuscript in the middle of his Bible, and inserted his fingers at the places where were to be found the passages of Scripture to be quoted in the reading of his sermon. This made it necessary to hold his Bible in both hands, and rendered all gesticulation with his hands impossible. As he proceeded he would read the passages of Scripture where his fingers were inserted, and thus liberate one finger after another until the fingers of both hands were read out of their places. When his fingers were all read out, he was near the close of the sermon. His reading was altogether unimpassioned and monotonous; and although the people attended very closely and reverentially to his reading, yet, I must confess, it was to me not much like preaching."

When Finney was teaching school in New Jersey, most of the preaching in his neighborhood was in German, and so he did not hear more than half a dozen sermons in English during his entire stay there, which was about three years. So when he went to Adams to study law he was almost as ignorant of religion as a heathen. He had been brought up mostly in the wilderness, had little regard for the Sabbath day, and had no definite knowledge of religious truth.

Not long after he went to Adams, however, Reverend George W. Gale, from Princeton, New Jersey, became pastor of the Presbyterian Church in that place. Gale was a Calvinist, and according to Finney, his preaching was "what has been called hyper-Calvinism." Although Finney listened carefully to him, he wasn't able to learn much from Gale. He said,

> "As I sometimes told him, he seemed to me to begin in the middle of his discourse, and to assume many things which to my mind needed to be proved. He seemed to take it for granted that his hearers were theologians, and therefore that he might assume all the great and fundamental doctrines of the Gospel. But I must say that I was more perplexed than edified by his preaching."

Up to this time Finney had never lived anyplace where he could attend a regular prayer meeting. But the Presbyterian Church near his office held one every week, so as often as he could get away from business he attended the meetings to listen to the prayers, although he did not pray himself.

While studying books on elementary law, Finney found that the old authors frequently quoted the Scriptures, and referred especially to the Mosaic Laws as authority for many of the great principles of common law. This aroused his curiosity, so he purchased the first Bible he had ever owned. Whenever he found a reference by the law authors to the Bible, he turned to the Scripture passage to see how it was connected to the common law. This led him to take a new interest in the Bible, and he read it and meditated upon its words more than he had ever done in his life. Much of it, however, he did not understand.

At that time, Reverend Gale was in the habit of dropping into his office to ask Finney what he thought about his previous Sunday's sermon. Finney talked freely with him, and brought up so many objections to Gale's positions that it forced Finney to think deeper about them. Finney said,

"In conversing with him and asking him questions, I perceived that his own mind was, as I thought, mystified; and that he did not accurately define to himself what he meant by many of the important terms that he used. Indeed I found it impossible to attach any meaning to many of the terms which he used with great formality and frequency. What did he mean by repentance? Was it a mere feeling of sorrow for sin? Was it altogether a passive state of mind, or did it involve a voluntary element? If it was a change of mind, in what respect was it a change of mind? What did he mean by the term regeneration? What did such language mean when applied to a spiritual change? What did he mean by faith? Was it merely an intellectual state? Was it merely a conviction, or persuasion, that the things stated in the Gospel were true? What did he mean by sanctification? Did it involve any physical change in the subject, or any physical influence on the part of God? I could not tell, nor did he seem to me to know himself, in what sense he used these and similar terms.

"We had a great many interesting conversations; but they seemed rather to stimulate my own mind to inquiry, than to satisfy me in respect to the truth.

"But as I read my Bible and attended the prayer meetings, heard Mr. Gale preach, and conversed with him, with the elders of the church, and with others from time to time, I became very restless. A little consideration convinced me that I was by no means in a state of mind to go to heaven if I should die. It seemed to me that there must be something in religion that was of infinite importance; and it was soon settled with me, that if the soul was immortal I needed a great change in my inward state to be prepared for happiness in heaven. But still my mind was not made up as to the truth or falsehood of the Gospel and of the Christian religion. The question, however, was of too much importance to allow me to rest in any uncertainty on the subject."

Finney was now regularly attending the weekly prayer meeting, and the thing that struck him most was that the people who prayed never got their prayers answered. In fact, it seemed to him that they did not expect to get their prayers answered, yet when he searched his Bible, which he was now doing almost constantly, he found an abundance of Scriptures in which God promised to answer prayers. He said,

"When I read my Bible I learned what Christ had said in regard to prayer, and answers to prayer. He had said, "Ask, and ye shall receive, seek and ye shall find, knock and it shall he opened unto you. For everyone that asketh receiveth, and he that seeketh findeth, and to him that knocketh it shall be opened." I read also what Christ affirms, that God is more willing to give His Holy Spirit to them that ask Him, than earthly parents are to give good gifts to their children. I heard them pray continually for the outpouring of the Holy Spirit, and often confess that they did not receive what they asked for.

"They exhorted each other to wake up and be engaged, and to pray earnestly for a revival of religion, asserting that if they did their duty, prayed for the outpouring of the Spirit, and were in earnest, that the Spirit of God would be poured out, that they would have a revival of religion, and that the impenitent would be converted. But in their prayer and conference meetings they would continually confess, substantially, that they were making no progress in securing a revival of religion.

"On one occasion, when I was in one of the prayer meetings, I was asked if I did not desire that they should pray for me! I told them, no; because I did not see that God answered their prayers. I said, 'I suppose I need to be prayed for, for I am conscious that I am a sinner; but I do not see that it will do any good for you to pray for me; for you are continually asking, but you do not receive. You have been praying for a revival of religion ever since I have been in Adams, and yet you have it not. You have been praying for the Holy Spirit to descend upon yourselves, and yet complaining of your leanness.' I recollect having used this expression at that time: 'You have prayed enough since I have attended these meetings to have prayed the devil out of Adams, if there is any virtue in your prayers. But here you are praying on, and complaining still.'"

As Finney continued studying the Bible he came to the conclusion that the reason their prayers were not answered was because they did not comply with the revealed conditions upon which God had promised to answer prayer; that they did not pray in faith, expecting God to give them the things that they asked for.

Finney continued struggling with this and many other concerns and questions for two or three years, and finally came to the conclusion that regardless of what seemed to be the lack of understanding in his mind or in his pastor's mind, or in the mind of the Church's congregation, the Bible was, nevertheless, the true Word of God.

Having come to that conclusion, Finney was now brought face to face with the question as to whether he would receive Jesus Christ as presented in the Gospel, or whether he would continue to live a worldly life. The Holy Spirit was now working so strongly with Finney that the thought was continually upon his mind, and he knew that he could not long leave the question unsettled, nor could he long hesitate between the lives presented to him—a spiritual life or a worldly life.

On a Sunday evening, October 8, 1821, Finney made up his mind that he would settle the question of his soul's salvation at once, that if it was possible he would make his peace with God. But still he seemed to hesitate. He was quite busy in his office and wasn't certain when he would find the time. Finally, he realized that unless he was resolute and firm in his decision, he would keep putting it off until it might be too late.

There was also a problem within himself that he had never before given any thought to, and it was that he was very proud without knowing it. He always thought that he did not have much regard or concern about the opinion of others, but he now found that he did not want anyone to know that he was seeking the salvation of his soul. Now when he prayed in his office, he would only pray in a whisper, and that after plugging in the keyhole in the doors so that no one could possibly see that he was engaged in prayer. And where he had previously always had his Bible lying on the table with his law books, he now laid his law books on top of it so that no one could see that he might possibly have been reading it. Previously he had been willing to talk to anyone about spiritual matters, and now he did not want to talk to anybody, especially about how he was feeling.

On Monday and Tuesday his convictions increased, but it seemed to him as if his heart was going harder instead of softer. He could not shed a tear, he could not pray above a whisper, and when he did pray he felt no relief. He became shy, avoided everyone, would not speak to anyone on any subject, and did everything to avoid any suspicion that he was seeking the salvation of his soul. Tuesday evening he became very nervous, and during the night a strange feeling came over him as if he was about to die. He knew

Finney's birthplace in Warren, Connecticut

Charles G. Finney at the beginning and the end of his ministry.

BIRTHPLACE OF
REV. CHARLES G. FINNEY
NOTED EVANGELIST
PRESIDENT OF OBERLIN COLLEGE
1851 TO 1866
BORN AUGUST 29, 1792
DIED AUGUST 16, 1875

Memorial plaque monument created by Oberlin College

that if he did he would sink down to hell, but he quieted himself as well as he could until morning.

Early in the morning he started for his office, but before he arrived there dozens of questions flooded his mind. Questions like these: "What are you waiting for? Did you not promise to give your heart to God? And what are you trying to do? Are you endeavoring to work out a righteousness of your own?"

Then the Holy Spirit suddenly opened the Gospel of salvation to him. This is what Finney wrote in his Memoirs about that moment.

Just at this point the whole question of Gospel salvation opened to my mind in a manner most marvelous to me at the time. I think I then saw, as clearly as I ever have in my life, the reality and fullness of the atonement of Christ. I saw that His work was a finished work; and that instead of having, or needing, any righteousness of my own to recommend me to God, I had to submit myself to the righteousness of God through Christ. Gospel salvation seemed to me to be an offer of something to be accepted; and that it was full and complete; and that all that was necessary on my part, was to get my own consent to give up my sins, and accept Christ. Salvation, it seemed to me, instead of being a thing to be wrought out, by my own works, was a thing to be found entirely in the Lord Jesus Christ, who presented Himself before me as my God and my Savior.

Without being distinctly aware of it, I had stopped in the street right where the inward voice seemed to arrest me. How long I remained in that position I cannot say. But after this distinct revelation had stood for some little time before my mind, the question seemed to be put, "Will you accept it now, today?" I replied, "Yes; I will accept it today, or I will die in the attempt."

North of the village, just over a small hill, there was a wooded area where Finney often walked in pleasant weather. Although it was now the 10th of October and past the time of the year for his frequent walks, he decided to go there so that he could be alone and pour out his heart to God without anyone seeing him. But now his pride showed up again, and he became concerned that someone might see him going into the woods to pray, although probably no one in the town would have thought of Finney doing such a thing. Yet he hid himself along a fence as well as he could until he reached the woods and then walked about a quarter of a mile into it until he was certain that no one from the road could see him. There he found a couple of large trees that had fallen against each other and formed a small enclosure. He crept into it and knelt down to pray.

When he decided to go into the woods he said to himself, "I will give my heart to God, or I never will come down from there." But now when he attempted to pray he found that he could not. He had thought that when he was certain no one could hear him he would be able to pray freely. But now he seemed to have nothing to say to God. And every time he heard a rustle in the leaves he would peek out of his enclosure to see if anyone was coming. This is what Finney wrote about the battle in his soul.

Finally I found myself verging fast to despair. I said to myself, "I cannot pray. My heart is dead to God, and will not pray." I then reproached myself for having promised to give my heart to God before I left the woods. When I came to try, I found I could not give my heart to God. My inward soul hung back, and there was no going out of my heart to God. I began to feel deeply that it was too late; that it must be that I was given up of God and was past hope.

Just at this moment I again thought I heard someone approach me, and I opened my eyes to see whether it were so. But right there the revelation of my pride of heart, as the great difficulty that stood in the way, was distinctly shown to me. An overwhelming sense of my wickedness in being ashamed to have a human being see me on my knees before God, took such powerful possession of me, that I cried at the top of my voice, and exclaimed that I would not leave that place if all the men on earth and all the devils in hell surrounded me. "What!" I said, "such a degraded sinner I am, on my knees confessing my sins to the great and holy God; and ashamed to have any human being, and a sinner like myself, find me on my knees endeavoring to make my peace with my offended God!" The sin appeared awful, infinite. It broke me down before the Lord.

Then Scriptures from the Old and New Testament began pouring through his mind, great and comforting promises of God for those who would believe in Jesus Christ. Many of them Finney could not recall ever having read or heard before, but he knew that they were the Word of God, and he knew that it was the Holy Spirit speaking to him about his soul. He cried out to Jesus Christ, "Lord, I take Thee at Thy word. Now Thou knowest that I do search for Thee with all my heart, and that I have come here to pray to Thee; and Thou hast promised to hear me."

Time passed as Finney prayed and the Holy Spirit continued to communicate to his soul. Finally he got up and headed out of the woods to the road. The thought of his being converted had not even entered his mind, and as he walked through the woods he said to himself, "If I am ever converted, I will preach the Gospel." When he reached the village he found that it was noon, although he had gone into the woods immediately after an early breakfast. He had been so absorbed in prayer that he had no idea of the time. There was now a great peace in his soul, and the burden of sin had completely rolled away. So much so that he was tempted to believe that he was not yet born of God. He went to eat dinner, but found that he had no appetite. He then went to the office and took down his bass viol and, as he had become accustomed to do, began to play and sing some pieces of sacred music, but his soul was so overflowing that he could not sing without weeping.

On the same evening of his conversion, without asking for it or even knowing that there was any such thing, Finney received a mighty baptism of the Holy Spirit. It was this baptism that brought to him the overwhelming convicting power of the Holy Spirit that poured through him whenever he talked to anyone about the condition of their soul and their need for salvation through Jesus Christ. It was this baptism of the Holy Spirit that made him what many consider to be the greatest revivalist that ever lived. Here is Finney's description of his baptism.

After dinner we [Finney and Squire Wright] were engaged in removing our books and furniture to another office. We were very busy in this, and had but little conversation all the afternoon. My mind, however, remained in that profoundly tranquil state. There was a great sweetness and tenderness in my thoughts and feelings. Everything appeared to be going right, and nothing seemed to ruffle or disturb me in the least.

Just before evening the thought took possession of my mind, that as soon as I was left alone in the new office, I would try to pray again—that I was not going to abandon the subject of religion and give it up, at any rate; and therefore, although I no longer had any concern about my soul, still I would continue to pray.

By evening we got the books and furniture adjusted; and I made up, in an open fireplace, a good fire, hoping to spend the evening alone. Just at dark, Squire Wright, seeing that everything was adjusted, bade me goodnight and went to his home. I had accompanied him to the door; and as I closed the door and turned around, my heart seemed to be liquid within me. All my feelings seemed to rise and flow out; and the utterance of my heart was, "I want to pour my whole soul out to God." The rising of my soul was so great that I rushed into the room back of the front office, to pray.

There was no fire, and no light, in the room; nevertheless it appeared to me as if it were perfectly light. As I went in and shut the door after me, it seemed as if I met the Lord Jesus Christ face to face. It did not occur to me then, nor did it for some time afterward, that it was wholly a mental state. On the contrary it seemed to me that I saw Him as I would see any other man. He said nothing, but looked at me in such a manner as to break me right down at his feet. I have always since regarded this as a most remarkable state of mind; for it seemed to me a reality, that He stood before me, and I fell down at his feet and poured out my soul to Him. I wept aloud like a child, and made such confessions as I could with my choked utterance. It seemed to me that I bathed His feet with my tears; and yet I had no distinct impression that I touched Him, that I recollect.

I must have continued in this state for a good while; but my mind was too much absorbed with the interview to recollect anything that I said. But I know, as soon as my mind became calm enough to break off from the interview, I returned to the front office, and found that the fire that I had made of large wood was nearly burned out. But as I turned and was about to take a seat by the fire, I received a mighty baptism of the Holy Ghost. Without any expectation of it, without ever having the thought in my mind that there was any such thing for me, without any recollection that I had ever heard the thing mentioned by any person in the world, the Holy Spirit descended upon me in a manner that seemed to go through me, body and soul. I could feel the impression, like a wave of electricity, going through and through me. Indeed it seemed to come in waves and waves of liquid love, for I could not express it in any other way. It seemed like the very breath of God. I can recollect distinctly that it seemed to fan me, like immense wings.

No words can express the wonderful love that was shed abroad in my heart. I wept aloud with joy and love; and I do not know but I should say, I literally bellowed out the unutterable gushings of my heart. These waves came over me, and over me, and over me, one after the other, until I recollect I cried out, "I shall die if these waves continue to pass over me." I said, "Lord, I cannot bear any more"; yet I had no fear of death.

Finney continued for some time under this remarkable baptism of the Holy Spirit. Wave after wave of spiritual power rolled over him and through him, thrilling and filling him. Later that evening a member of his choir—for he was the leader of the choir—came into the office. He was a member of the church, but was astonished to see Finney weeping under the power of the Spirit. After asking a few questions, he went to get an elder of the church who was a very serious man. When the elder saw Finney weeping under the Spirit's power he laughed so hard it seemed as though it was impossible for him to stop. A young man who was associated with Finney came into the office while Finney was trying to relate his experience to the elder and the member of the choir. He listened with astonishment to what Finney was saying, and suddenly fell upon the floor and cried out in the greatest agony of mind, "Do pray for me!" They all prayed for him and then the others went home and left Finney alone.

Although Finney had received a remarkable manifestation of the baptism of the Holy Spirit, still he doubted that he had received the true baptism, especially since Elder B. had laughed so hilariously when Finney told him what was happening to him. So regardless of the baptism that he received, this temptation to doubt was so strong that he went to bed uncertain that he had made peace with God. But God did not leave him long in that state of uncertainty.

I soon fell asleep, but almost as soon awoke again on account of the great flow of the love of God that was in my heart. I was so filled with love that I could not sleep. Soon I fell asleep again, and awoke in the same manner. When I awoke, this temptation would return upon me, and the love that seemed to be in my heart would abate; but as soon as I was asleep, it was so warm within me that I would immediately awake. Thus I continued till, late at night, I obtained some sound repose.

When I awoke in the morning the sun had risen, and was pouring a clear light into my room. Words cannot express the impression that this sunlight made upon me. Instantly the baptism that I had received the night before returned upon me in the same manner. I arose upon my knees in the bed and wept aloud with joy, and remained for some time too much overwhelmed with the baptism of the Spirit to do anything but pour out my soul to God. It seemed as if this morning's baptism was accompanied with a gentle reproof, and the Spirit seemed to say to me, "Will you doubt? Will you doubt?" I cried, "No! I will not doubt; I cannot doubt." He then cleared the subject up so much to my mind that it was in fact impossible for me to doubt that the Spirit of God had taken possession of my soul.

It was in this way that God taught Finney the doctrine of justification by faith as a present experience. He had never before seen it as a fundamental doctrine of the Gospel, indeed he did not really know what justification meant. But he could now see and understand what was meant by the passage, "being justified by faith, we have peace with God through our Lord Jesus Christ." He saw that the moment he believed while in the woods, all sense of condemnation had dropped out of his mind, and from that moment he could not feel any guilt or condemnation, no matter how much he tried. His sins were gone, and he had no more sense of guilt than if he had never sinned.

This was just the revelation that Finney needed. He felt himself justified by faith, and, so far as he could see, he was in a state in which he did not sin. Instead of feeling that he was sinning all the time, his heart was so full of love that it overflowed. His cup ran over with blessing and with love, and he could not feel that he was sinning against God. Nor could he recover the least sense of guilt for his past sins. It was what he had been looking for ever since he had believed that the Bible was the true Word of God.

Waves of power and love continued to flow over Finney even when he went to his office that morning. When Squire Wright came into the office, Finney said a few words to him on the subject of salvation. The words pierced him like an arrow and without replying he dropped his head, and a few minutes later he left the office. In the days that followed several persons were converted in the woods, and when Squire Wright heard them tell about their experience he resolved that he would never go to the woods to pray. To him it seemed unnecessary, he could be saved anyplace of his own choosing. He said, "I have a parlor to pray in. I am not going to the woods."

Weeks passed by and Squire Wright's convictions deepened. He tried to persuade himself that it was not pride that kept him from Christ, and so when he would be going home from a church meeting he would kneel in the street and pray. He would even look about for a mud puddle in which to pray, to show that he had no pride in the matter, but still no peace came. Realizing at last that pride was, nevertheless, the great obstacle in the way of his salvation he decided to yield. On going to the woods and kneeling down to pray he was filled with such a sense of peace and joy that he was almost overcome.

Although he loved the law, Finney now lost all taste for it, and for any other secular business. All he wanted to do now was preach the Gospel and win souls to Christ. Nothing else mattered to him. About that day Finney wrote,

> Soon after Mr. Wright had left the office, Deacon B came into the office and said to me, "Mr. Finney, do you recollect that my cause is to be tried at ten o'clock this morning? I suppose you are ready?" I had been retained to attend this suit as his attorney. I replied to him, "Deacon B, I have a retainer from the Lord Jesus Christ to plead His cause, and I cannot plead yours." He looked at me with astonishment, and said, "What do you mean?" I told him, in a few words, that I had enlisted in the cause of Christ; and then repeated that I had a retainer from the Lord Jesus Christ to plead His cause, and that he must go and get somebody else to attend his lawsuit; I could not do it. He dropped his head, and without making any reply, went out. A few moments later, in passing the window, I observed that Deacon B was standing in the road, seemingly lost in deep meditation. He went away, as I afterward learned, and immediately settled his suit. He then betook himself to prayer, and soon got into a much higher religious state than he had ever been in before.

Finney left his office that day and went out to talk to individuals concerning the salvation of their souls. Almost every person he spoke to was stricken with conviction of sin and soon afterwards received Christ as Lord and Savior. His words seemed to pierce their hearts like arrows. Among those brought to Christ through his efforts that day were a Universalist and a distiller.

During the day there was a great deal of conversation and excitement about Finney's conversion, and in the evening most of the people in the village gathered at the church, although no meeting had been scheduled so far as Finney could learn. All the people seemed to be waiting for him to speak, and he got up and told what the Lord had done for his soul. A certain Mr. C, who was present, was so convicted of sin that he jumped up and rushed out and went home, leaving his hat behind. Many others were also deeply convicted of sin. Finney spoke and prayed with liberty, although he had never prayed in public before. The meeting was a wonderful one, and several people were convicted of their sins and received Jesus Christ. After that day, meetings were held every night for some time. The revival spread among everyone in the village and to many surrounding places. All of Finney's former companions, except for one, received Christ.

Not long after his conversion Finney visited his parents at Henderson. His father met him at the gate, saying, "How do you do, Charles?" to which he replied: "I am very well, father, body and soul. But father, you are an old man; all of your children have grown up and have left your house; and I never heard a prayer in my father's house." His father dropped his head and burst into tears saying: "I know it, Charles. Come in and pray yourself." He did so, with the result that his father and mother were deeply moved and soon after both were converted. He remained in town for two or three days talking with everybody he met about the great theme of salvation. Within a week a meeting was started in the town, and a revival soon followed. "From this meeting," said Finney, "the work of the Lord spread forth in every direction all over the town. And thus it spread at that time from Adams as a center, throughout nearly all the towns in the county."

During these early months of his Christian life, Finney was in an almost constant attitude of devotion, and had many days of fasting and prayer, when he would separate himself entirely from others, and seek a closer communion with God. These days of fasting and prayer were not all of them equally profitable. He soon learned that his motives could not be purified, nor his faith increased, by mere self-examination. Sometimes this process brought nothing but darkness to him and almost destroyed his affections for God. It was only as he turned his thoughts towards Christ and His work that his affections and pious resolutions were strengthened. His longing after God was so deep that if anything interrupted his sense of the divine presence, he found it impossible to rest, or to study, or to derive the least satisfaction from anything he was doing. He was constantly impelled by an overwhelming desire to seek reconciliation with God, which he felt was an indispensable preparation for his daily work of speaking to others about Christ.

By the spring of the next year, 1822, the older members of Finney's church began to markedly decline in their involvement and zeal for God. This greatly oppressed Finney, as it did also the young converts generally. About this time he read in a newspaper an article under the head of, "A Revival Revived." The substance of it was that in a certain place there had been a revival during the winter and that in the spring it declined. But when earnest prayer was offered for the continued outpouring of the Spirit, the revival was powerfully revived. This article set Finney into a flood of weeping.

He was at that time boarding with Mr. Gale, and he took the article to him. Finney was so overcome with a sense of God's divine goodness in hearing and answering prayer, and with a felt assurance that He would hear and answer prayer for the revival of His work in Adams, that he went through the house weeping aloud like a child. Mr. Gale seemed surprised at his feelings, and his expressed confidence that God would revive His work. The article made no such impression on this to Gale as it did on Finney.

At the next meeting of the young people, Finney proposed that they should observe a closet concert of prayer for the revival of God's work—that they should pray at sunrise, at noon, and at sunset, in their closets, and continue this for one week. At that time they would come together again and see what further was to be done. No other means were used for the revival of God's work. But the spirit of prayer was immediately poured out wonderfully upon the young converts. Before the week was out, Finney learned that some of them, when they would attempt to observe this season of prayer, would lose all their strength and be unable to rise to their feet, or even kneel in their closets. Others could only lie prostrate on the floor and pray with unutterable groanings for the outpouring of the Spirit of God.

The Spirit was poured out, and before the week ended all the meetings were thronged; and there was as much interest in religion as there had been at any time during the revival.

Not long after receiving the baptism with the Holy Spirit, Finney had a long conversation with his pastor, Reverend Gale, about his preparing for the ministry. Gale was a graduate of Princeton University, and was a firm believer in hyper-Calvinistic doctrines, which to Finney's mind seemed absurd and contradictory. He and Gale could barely agree on any point of doctrine. Gale believed in the doctrine of a limited atonement, or that Christ died only for the elect, while Finney believed that He died for all. Gale believed that people were so depraved by nature that they had no free will, while Finney believed that everyone had the power to accept or reject salvation.

Regardless of their differences, in the spring of 1822 Finney placed himself under the care of the Presbytery as a candidate for the ministry. Some of the ministers urged him to go to Princeton, but he said he did not have the time nor the inclination. They then appointed Reverend Gale to supervise his studies, which as far as Mr. Gale was concerned were only a series of controversies. But Finney did make good use of Gale's library. He felt, however, that he would rather not preach than teach the doctrines held by Gale.

Fortunately, there was one member of the church to whom Finney could open his mind freely on the subject of salvation; a man whom Finney identified as Elder H, a very godly, praying man. He had been educated at Princeton, and held strongly to the higher doctrines of Calvinism that were taught there. Nevertheless, he and Finney had frequent and protracted conversations, and he became satisfied that Finney was right. Elder H called on Finney frequently to have seasons of prayer with him, to strengthen him in his studies, and in his discussions with Mr. Gale, and to help him decide more and more firmly that, come what may, he would preach the Gospel.

The Presbytery was finally called together at Adams in 1824 and licensed Finney to preach. The two written sermons he prepared for them were, with two exceptions, the only written sermons he ever prepared. He tried one other time to preach from a written sermon, but believed that it hindered the Spirit of God from speaking through him. Finney not only worked out his own system of theology, based as it was upon his prayerful and independent study of the Scriptures interpreted in the light of the vivid religious experience through which he had passed, but he had his own notions as to how the Gospel should be preached. Written sermons at that time were the order of the day, but Finney preached as he would when addressing a jury. "What would be thought of a lawyer," he asked, "who should stand up before a jury and read an essay to them? He would lose his case!"

Just as an attorney sought to win a verdict for his client, so he aimed at bringing lost souls to a decision for Jesus Christ. He was God's advocate, pleading with sinners to turn from the error of their ways and accept the offered gift of salvation. He sought to convert people by the truth, and like Paul of old he "reasoned of righteousness, temperance, and judgment to come." His preaching was highly logical and analytical. In fact, his critics said that he had a great tendency to go to excess in this area, his sermons sometimes having as high as forty to fifty divisions. These divisions often consisted of a single sentence, but the thought was so clear and the applications so logical that the most simple statement went like an arrow to its mark.

Finney sought to express his thoughts in simple language so that everyone might understand his message. His illustrations, like the Lord's, were drawn from the ordinary activities of life. He said, "When I came to preach the Gospel, my mind was so anxious to be thoroughly understood, that I studied in the most earnest manner, on the one hand to avoid what was vulgar, and on the other to express my thought with the greatest simplicity of language."

His manner of delivery was colloquial and repetitious. He often argued truths that seemed to need no further argument, and repeated statements that apparently had been taken for granted. He said: "I talked to the people as I would have talked to a jury. Of all the causes that were ever plead, the cause of religion, I thought, had the fewest able advocates, and that if advocates at the bar should pursue the same course in pleading the cause of their clients that ministers do in pleading the cause of Christ with sinners, they would not gain a single case."

He was often criticized for his lawyer-like method of presenting the truth and for lowering the dignity of the pulpit. But to his hearers it seemed as if he were talking to them personally about matters of great mutual concern. Those who heard him often said: "Why it didn't seem like preaching. It seemed as if Mr. Finney had taken me alone, and was conversing with me face to face."

Where most preachers in those days spoke of sin in general and rarely, if ever, directed their preaching at the congregation, Finney made his preaching as personal as he could. If Finney were in some place new, he would often walk throughout the area during the day and listen to the people, especially to the men who often used profane and blasphemous language. Then during the meeting he would detail what he had seen and heard, and press the specific sins of the people upon them.

He wrote this about a meeting in Antwerp, just north of Evans Mills: "I saw several of the men there from whom I had, the day before, heard the most awful profanity. I pointed them out in the meeting, and told what they said, how they called on God to damn each other. Indeed, I let loose my whole heart upon them. I told them they seemed to howl blasphemy about the streets like hell-hounds; and it seemed to me that I had arrived on the very verge of hell. Everybody knew that what I said was true, and they quailed under it. They did not appear offended; but the people wept about as much as I did myself. I think there were scarcely any dry eyes in the house."

Finney's preaching was like a sledgehammer, breaking down every excuse they had, striking at them again and again, leaving them no way to escape its blows. Indeed, most of his preaching resulted in the same effect that Peter's did on the day of Pentecost when the hearts of the people were pierced, and they said, "What must we do to be saved?"

Finney's first regular meetings were held at Evans Mills, Oneida County, New York. Here is what Finney himself had to say about the meetings.

I began, as I said, to preach in the stone schoolhouse at Evans Mills. The people were very much interested, and thronged the place to hear me preach. They extolled my preaching; and the little Congregational church became very much interested, and hopeful that they should be built up, and that there would be a revival. More or less convictions occurred under every sermon that I preached; but still no general conviction appeared upon the public mind.

I was very much dissatisfied with this state of things; and at one of my evening services, after having preached there two or three Sabbaths, and several evenings in the week, I told the people at the close of my sermon, that I had come there to secure the salvation of their souls; that my preaching, I knew, was highly complimented by them; but that, after all, I did not come there to please them but to bring them to repentance; that it mattered not to me how well they were pleased with my preaching, if after all they rejected my Master; that something was wrong, either in me or in them; that the kind of interest they manifested in my preaching was doing them no good; and that I could not spend my time with them unless they were going to receive the Gospel. I then, quoting the words of Abraham's servant, said to them, "Now will you deal kindly and truly with my master? If you will, tell me; and if not, tell me, that I may turn to the right hand or to the left."

I turned this question over, and pressed it upon them, and insisted upon it that I must know what course they proposed to pursue. If they did not purpose to become Christians, and enlist in the service of the Savior, I wanted to know it that I might not labor with them in vain. I said to them, "You admit that what I preach is the Gospel. You profess to believe it. Now will you receive it? Do you mean to receive it, or do you intend to reject it? You must have some mind about it. And now I have a right to take it for granted, in as much as you admit that I have preached the truth, that you acknowledge your obligation at once to become Christians. This obligation you do not deny; but will you meet the obligation? Will you discharge it? Will you do what you admit you ought to do? If you will not, tell me; and if you will, tell me, that I may turn to the right hand or to the left."

After turning this over till I saw they understood it well, and looked greatly surprised at my manner of putting it, I then said to them, "Now I must know your minds, and I want you who have made up your minds to become Christians, and will give your pledge to make your peace with God immediately, to rise up. But I want those of you who are resolved that you will not become Christians, and wish me so to understand, and wish Christ so to understand, to sit still." After making this plain, so that I knew that they understood it, I then said: "You who are now willing to pledge to me and to Christ, that you will immediately make your peace with God, please rise up. On the contrary, you that mean that I should understand that you are committed to remain in your present attitude, not to accept Christ—those of you that are of this mind, may sit still." They looked at one another and at me, and all sat still just as I expected.

After looking around upon them for a few moments, I said, "Then you are committed. You have taken your stand. You have rejected Christ and His Gospel; and ye are witnesses one against the other, and God is witness against you all. This is explicit and you may remember as long as you live, that you have thus publicly committed yourselves against the Savior, and said, 'We will not have this man, Christ Jesus, to reign over us.'" This is the purport of what I urged upon them, and as nearly in these words as I can recollect.

When I thus pressed them they began to look angry, and arose, en masse, and started for the door. When they began to move, I paused. As soon as I stopped speaking they turned to see why I did not go on. I said, "I am sorry for you; and will preach to you once more, the Lord willing, tomorrow night."

No one had ever preached to them like this before, and although some of the deacons told Finney that no one would be back for the next meeting, one of the deacons said to him, "Brother Finney, you have got them. They cannot rest under this, rely upon it. The brethren are all discouraged," said he, "but I am not. I believe you have done the very thing that needed to be done, and that we shall see the results." And back they were. The church building overflowed, with people standing outside trying to get in. Finney preached just as hard at them again. He assumed that they were still in their rebellious condition, and at the end of the meeting dismissed them without giving them a chance to receive Christ.

Some were so angry they said they would never be back again, some threatened to shoot Finney, some were struck so hard that they couldn't even speak. The power of the Holy Spirit was moving, and it continued to move until revival broke out, and woe be to anyone who opposed the revival. "There was one old man in this place," Finney said, "who was not only an infidel, but a great railer at religion. He was very angry at the revival movement. I heard every day of his railing and blaspheming, but took no public notice of it. He refused altogether to attend meetings. But in the midst of his opposition, and when his excitement was great, while sitting one morning at the table, he suddenly fell out of his chair in a fit of apoplexy. A physician was immediately called, who, after a brief examination, told him that he could live but a very short time; and that if he had anything to say, he must say it at once. He had just strength and time, as I was informed, to stammer out, 'Don't let Finney pray over my corpse.' This was the last of his opposition in that place."

During the revival at Antwerp, an old man asked Finney to preach in a schoolhouse about three miles away. Finney said he would go there that Monday at five o'clock in the afternoon. When he arrived, he found the schoolhouse full. After some singing that was so discordant that Finney had to cover both ears with his hands, he threw himself to his knees, and "The Lord opened the windows of heaven, and the spirit of prayer was poured out, and I let my whole heart out in prayer."

Finney had not thought about the text he was going to preach, but waited to see the congregation. As soon as he had finished praying, he arose from his knees and said, "Up, get you out of this place; for the Lord will destroy this city." He told them he could not remember exactly where the verse was but gave them some idea where to find it, and then began to explain it.

As he told them about Abraham and Lot and the city of Sodom, and how wicked Sodom was and that Lot was the only righteous man in the city, and how the Lord sent Angels down to destroy the city and save Lot, he noticed that the people seemed to be getting increasingly angry. Listen to what he wrote in his Memoirs.

Many of the men were in their shirt sleeves; and they looked at each other and at me, as if they were ready to fall upon me and chastise me on the spot. I saw their strange and unaccountable looks, and could not understand what I was saying that had offended them. However it seemed to me that their anger rose higher and higher, as I continued the narrative. As soon as I had finished the narrative, I turned upon them and said that I understood that they had never had a religious meeting in that place; and that therefore I had a right to take it for granted, and was compelled to take it for granted, that they were an ungodly people. I pressed that home upon them with more and more energy, with my heart full almost to bursting.

I had not spoken to them in this strain of direct application, I should think, more than a quarter of an hour, when all at once an awful solemnity seemed to settle down upon them; the congregation began to fall from their seats in every direction, and cried for mercy. If I had had a sword in each hand, I could not have cut them off their seats as fast as they fell. Indeed nearly the whole congregation were either on their knees or prostrate, I should think, in less than two minutes from this first shock that fell upon them. Every one prayed for himself, who was able to speak at all.

Of course I was obliged to stop preaching; for they no longer paid any attention. I saw the old man who had invited me there to preach, sitting about in the middle of the house, and looking around with utter amazement. I raised my voice almost to a scream, to make him hear, and pointing to him said, "Can't you pray?" He instantly fell upon his knees, and with a stentorian voice poured himself out to God; but he did not at all get the attention of the people. I then spoke as loud as I could, and tried to make them attend to me. I said to them, "You are not in hell yet; and now let me direct you to Christ." For a few moments I tried to hold forth the Gospel to them; but scarcely any of them paid any attention. My heart was so overflowing with joy at such a scene that I could hardly contain myself. It was with much difficulty that I refrained from shouting, and giving glory to God.

As soon as I could sufficiently control my feelings I turned to a young man who was close to me, and was engaged in praying for himself, laid my hand on his shoulder, thus getting his attention, and preached in his ear Jesus. As soon as I got his attention to the Cross of Christ, he believed, was calm and quiet for a minute or two, and then broke out in praying for the others. I then turned to another, and took the same course with him, with the same result; and then another, and another.

In this way I kept on, until I found the time had arrived when I must leave them, and go and fulfill an appointment in the village. I told them this, and asked the old man who had invited me there, to remain and take charge of the meeting, while I went to my appointment. He did so. But there was too much interest, and there were too many wounded souls, to dismiss the meeting; and so it was held all night. In the morning there were still those there that could not get away; and they were carried to a private house in the neighborhood, to make room for the school. In the afternoon they sent for me to come down there, as they could not yet break up the meeting.

When I went down the second time, I got an expla-nation of the anger manifested by the congregation during the introduction of my sermon the day before. I learned that the place was called Sodom, but I knew it not; and that there was but one pious man in the place, and him they called Lot. This was the old man that invited me there. The people supposed that I had chosen my subject, and preached to them in that manner, because they were so wicked as to be called Sodom. This was a striking coincidence; but so far as I was concerned, it was altogether accidental.

Finney continued to preach the Gospel with increasing power and results. Most of his meetings were in the northeastern part of the United States, but he also traveled as far away as England with the same revival results there. For the continuance of the spiritual power that moved through him, Finney depended entirely upon his personal fasting and prayer and upon the prayers of others. He found that whenever the spirit of prayer left him, the convicting power of the Holy Spirit also left him. Whenever that happened, he would redouble his prayer efforts and the power would return. For years, a great man of prayer whom Finney referred to as Father or Brother Nash would occasionally attend Finney's meetings. Whenever he showed up, Finney knew that revival would soon follow. He was a great help to Finney in many of his meetings, and Finney wrote this about him concerning a local church that was opposing the meetings and had caused the young men in the area to set themselves strongly against conversion the way Finney preached it.

In this state of things, Brother Nash and myself, after consultation, made up our minds that that thing must be overcome by prayer, and that it could not be reached in any other way. We therefore retired to a grove and gave ourselves up to prayer until we prevailed, and we felt confident that no power which earth or hell could interpose, would be allowed permanently to stop the revival.

The next Sabbath, after preaching morning and afternoon myself—for I did the preaching altogether, and Brother Nash gave himself up almost continually to prayer—we met at five o'clock in the church, for a prayer meeting. The meeting house was filled. Near the close of the meeting, Brother Nash arose, and addressed that company of young men who had joined hand in hand to resist the revival. I believe they were all there, and they sat braced up against the Spirit of God. It was too solemn for them really to make ridicule of what they heard and saw; and yet their brazen-facedness and stiff-neckedness were apparent to everybody.

Brother Nash addressed them very earnestly, and pointed out the guilt and danger of the course they were taking. Toward the close of his address, he waxed exceeding warm, and said to them, "Now, mark me, young men! God will break your ranks in less than one week, either by converting some of you, or by sending some of you to hell. He will do this as certainly as the Lord is my God!" He was standing where he brought his hand down on the top of the pew before him, so as to make it thoroughly jar. He sat immediately down, dropped his head, and groaned with pain.

The house was as still as death, and most of the people held down their heads. I could see that the young men were agitated. For myself, I regretted that Brother Nash had gone so far. He had committed himself, that God would either take the life of some of them, and send them to hell, or convert some of them, within a week. However on Tuesday morning of the same week, the leader of these young men came to me, in the greatest distress of mind. He was all prepared to submit; and as soon as I came to press him he broke down like a child, confessed, and manifestly gave himself to Christ. Then he said, "What shall I do,

Mr. Finney?" I replied "Go immediately to all your young companions, and pray with them, and exhort them at once to turn to the Lord." He did so; and before the week was out, nearly if not all of that class of young men, were hoping in Christ.

Sometimes the power of God was so strong in Finney's meetings that almost the entire audience fell on their knees in prayer, or were prostrated on the floor, overwhelmed by the convicting power of the Holy Spirit. Sometimes when Finney was in the pulpit, he felt as if the power of the Holy Spirit had almost lifted him off his feet. Although many people did not believe that manifestations of the Holy Spirit's power would accompany the Spirit's moral work, in almost every Finney meeting when the moral work was deep and powerful, when people were strongly convicted of their sins and of judgment, there were physical manifestations of the power of the Holy Spirit.

There are reports that in several major cities in New York State, when Finney was holding meetings—cities like Syracuse, Rochester, Utica, Albany—a holy power would seem to settle upon the entire city. Salesmen traveling through the city by train told of being convicted of their sins as they sat in their railroad car. At times, visitors to the cities would be drawn to his meetings even though they did not know that meetings were being held. Sometimes sinners were brought under conviction of sin almost as soon as they entered a city where revival had broken out.

As revivals continued, the convicting power of the Holy Spirit so poured through Finney that people were often brought under conviction just by his presence. One notable example took place in a cotton mill near the village of Whitesboro, about 4 miles west of Utica where Finney was living. Here is Finney's record of it.

There was a cotton manufactory on the Oriskany creek, a little above Whitesboro, a place now called New York Mills. It was owned by a Mr. W, an unconverted man, but a gentleman of high standing and good morals. My brother-in-law, Mr. G A, was at that time superintendent of the factory. I was invited to go and preach at that place, and went up one evening, and preached in the village school-house, which was large, and was crowded with hearers. The Word, I could see, took powerful effect among the people, especially among the young people who were at work in the factory.

The next morning, after breakfast, I went into the factory, to look through it. As I went through, I observed there was a good deal of agitation among those who were busy at their looms, and their mules, and other implements of work. On passing through one of the apartments, where a great number of young women were attending to their weaving, I observed a couple of them eyeing me, and speaking very earnestly to each other; and I could see that they were a good deal agitated, although they both laughed. I went slowly toward them. They saw me coming, and were evidently much excited. One of them was trying to mend a broken thread, and I observed that her hands trembled so that she could not mend it.

I approached slowly, looking on each side at the machinery, as I passed; but observed that this girl grew more and more agitated, and could not proceed with her work. When I came within eight or ten feet of her, I looked solemnly at her. She observed it, and was quite overcome, and sunk down, and burst into tears. The impression caught almost like powder, and in a few moments nearly all in the room were in tears.

This feeling spread through the factory. Mr. W, the owner of the establishment, was present, and seeing the state of things, he said to the superintendent, "Stop the mill, and let the people attend to religion; for it is more important that our souls should be saved than that this factory run." The gate was immediately shut down, and the factory stopped; but where should we assemble? The superintendent suggested that the mule room was large; and, the mules being run up, we could assemble there. We did so, and a more powerful meeting I scarcely ever attended. It went on with great power. The building was large, and had many people in it, from the garret to the cellar. The revival went through the mill with astonishing power, and in the course of a few days nearly all in the mill were hopefully converted.

Finney was active in two Great American Awakenings. What has been called the Second Great American Awakening in the 1830s and 1840s, and the Third Great American Awakening, which was a revival in 1858-1859. The great revival of 1858-1859, which was brought to a halt by the Civil War, was said to be one of the greatest revivals in the world's history, and was a direct result of Finney's revival meetings. Dr. Lyman Beecher said, "That was the greatest work of God, and the greatest revival of religion the world has ever seen." It has been estimated that 600,000 people were bought to Christ in this revival.

Finney was married three times. The first time in 1824 to Lydia Root Andrews—she died in 1847. In 1848 he married Mrs. Elizabeth Ford Atkinson—she died in 1863. In 1864 he married Rebecca Rayl—she died in 1907.

In 1851, Finney was elected president of Oberlin College, located in what was then a wilderness in northern Ohio. He remained president until he resigned in 1865. Although no longer president, he continued to preach and lecture to the students at Oberlin until two weeks before his 83rd birthday.

Charles Grandison Finney had the longest sustained period of revivals of any minister in Christian history. From the first day of his conversion in 1821 and continuing through his time as president of Oberlin College there were almost constant revivals. Whenever there was a period of time when there was not a revival, Finney would go to prayer until the spirit of prayer came upon him and soon revival would break out. He did not, however, depend upon his prayers alone but would always solicit prayer from anyone and everyone around him whom he knew also had a spirit of prayer and a heart for revival. The prayers never failed, revival always came.

In his Memoirs he wrote this about his revival work at Oberlin College:

Our fall term is properly our harvest here. It begins about the first of September, when we have a large number of new students, and many of these unconverted ones. I have always felt, as a good many others have, and I believe the faculty generally, that during that term was the time to secure the conversion of our new students. This was secured to a very great extent, the year that we returned. The idea that during term time we could not expect a revival of religion, seemed to be exploded, the people took hold of the work and we had a powerful revival.

Since then we have been much less hindered in our revival efforts in term time, by counteracting influences, than we had been for a few years before. Our revival efforts have taken effect among the students from year to year, because they were aimed to secure the conversion especially of the students. Our general population is a changing one, and we very frequently need a sweeping revival through the whole town, among the householders as well as the students, to keep up a healthy tone of piety. A goodly number of our students learn to work themselves in promoting revivals, and are very efficient in laboring for the conversion of their fellow students. The young men's prayer meetings have been greatly blessed. The young people's meetings, where all meet for a general prayer meeting, have also been blessed. The efforts of brethren and sisters in the church have been increasingly blessed from year to year. We have had more or less of a revival continually, summer and winter.

Last winter, 1866 and 67, the revival was more powerful among the inhabitants [of the town] than it had been since 1860. However, as heretofore, I broke down in the midst, and was unable to attend any more meetings. The brethren, however, went forward with the work, and it continued with great interest until spring. Thus I have brought my revival narrative down to this time, the 13th of January, 1868.

Finney died on October 16, 1875. His last day on earth was a peaceful Sunday, which he had enjoyed with his family. At sunset he walked with his wife to listen to the music at the opening of the evening service in the church near his home. The worshipers were singing "Jesus, lover of my soul." He joined with them and sang to the end of the song. That night when he went to bed he had chest pains. About two o'clock in the morning he asked for some water. But it did not quench his thirst, and he said, "Perhaps this is the thirst of death." A moment later he added, "I am dying." Those were his last words.

Daniel 12:3 says, "And they that be wise shall shine as the brightness of the firmament; and they that turn many to righteousness as the stars for ever and ever." Surely no star will shine brighter than Charles Grandison Finney, the greatest revivalist the world has ever known.

Charles G. Finney tombstone located in Westwood Cemetery, Oberlin, Ohio

1

THE COMMUNICABLE SECRET OF MR. FINNEY'S POWER

By Arthur Tappan Pierson

[Note. The following is a substantial reproduction of an address at the Memorial Meeting, which was not written until since its delivery. A.T.P.]

As we study the life of any man of mark, we see some traits that stand out boldly, like mountains in a landscape, and give individuality, idiosyncrasy and sometimes idiosyncraziness. They distinguish the man from all others, and remind us of the famous couplet of Byron's:

"Nature formed but one such man,
And broke the die, in moulding Sheridan."

If these traits were all, biography could serve us but little; in our proneness to shirk heroic effort, we should say of such men, 'they are inimitable,' and rest content with our low level of life.

No doubt, some secrets of Mr. Finney's success are incommunicable, such as his insight into human nature, his powers of analysis and argument, physical and nervous energy, vivid imagination, rapidity of thought and speech, and athletic vigor in antagonism. But are we to stand afar off, and view his devotion to God and to souls, with an awe that dismisses all thought of imitation or emulation?

If so, that life has left its print upon the living leaves of history, largely in vain. Upon Life's Field of the Cloth of Gold, God has flung a knightly gauntlet, challenging us all to a true Christian chivalry! Mr. Finney shows us, on a grand scale, what one life may be and do; and were he here, he would say, with Paul, "Be ye followers of me, even as I also am of Christ."

In speaking of the communicable secrets of his power, we begin and end with the ultimate source of all power, namely, Character. As a man, Mr. Finney was specially marked by Candor, Courage, Conscientiousness, and Consecration.

Candor is no common virtue. Few men are honest with themselves; they evade and avoid convictions that would compel them to condemn their past course and reform their present practices. He was habitually honest with himself, with God, and with men. His was a candid mind that rejoices in the truth, even when it rebukes, and that must deal honestly, whether in searching self, praying to God, or speaking to men. His frankness surprised and sometimes offended; but a second sober thought led men to feel that he who told them the plain truth was the man to go to, when they sought salvation or sanctification.

His Courage was not of that physical type which is often only the consciousness and confidence of brute-force; but it was moral intrepidity. It made him bold to face and fight wrong doctrine or bad practice. He was decisive and incisive in dealing with souls;

regardless of conventional restraints; daring in his blows at popular idols; brave in the use of any means that he believed right and effective. Such courage came from that conscious fellowship with God, which made Luther bold as a lion before the Diet of Worms, gave Knox his motto, "One with God is a majority," and led Paul to ask, "If God be for us, who can be against us?"

His Conscientiousness was seen in instant and constant obedience to every conviction of duty, whether it came through his moral sense, the Written Word, or the living spirit. To know the right was to pursue it; to perceive the truth was to receive it; to see God's will was to submit to it, in serving or in suffering. He proved that "God hath given" the Holy Ghost "to them that obey Him" (Acts 5:32); for, while others passively waited for the Spirit to imbue and endue them, he learned that each new act of obedience brought a new baptism.

His Consecration was the laying of himself as a whole offering on God's altar. Emptying himself of selfish ambition, he held up the emptied vessel to be filled with the grace of God. Moreover, the "tabernacle" which he thus "sanctified to God's glory," God "sanctified by His glory." Mr. Finney found many disciples, who, like those whom Paul found at Ephesus, had not received, or so much as heard of, the Holy Ghost, since they believed. These had got as far as John's baptism of repentance, but not as far as Jesus' baptism of spiritual life and power. He taught the Church to go on from the grace of salvation to that of sanctification, and still on to that of service, that each believer might be "a vessel, sanctified and made meet for the Master's use, prepared unto every good work."

Thus far, Mr. Finney's example is not certainly beyond the reach of imitation. But may we attain unto his great Faith? How did that faith come to be so great? Was it conferred outright, as a gift of God, or was it cultivated?

We answer that his faith fed and grew upon the Word of God. He searched his Bible on his knees, and grouped its promises, until unbelief fell, smitten, before the combined blaze of their testimony. It grew, again, by the experience of prayer. Experiment is the most convincing argument. God bids the doubting soul, "Enter into thy closet;" there "handle me and see!" there "prove me, if I will not open you the windows of heaven and pour you out a blessing till there be none left to pour out." Faith is confirmed by every new promise that the prayerful soul grasps, and especially by every new experience of prayer answered.

Was Mr. Finney's power as a preacher, in any measure communicable? Here again we note four imitable qualities: he was simple, sincere, scriptural, and spiritual.

His simplicity was seen in his singleness of aim, his sacred zeal to glorify God in saving and sanctifying souls. He cared more for the groan of one whom the arrow of truth had wounded, than for the shouts of an hundred praising the archer's skill. To reach and touch that which is deepest and most abiding in man was what he sought; not to play on transient sensibilities and emotions, but to mould lasting convictions, affections, and resolutions.

Hence he avoided dogmatism, substituted argument for authority, assumed nothing, and led the mind on, step by step, to the embrace of truth. Then he struck for the Will. While the iron was at white heat, he brought down the hammer to give it shape; with awful emphasis on personal responsibility and the obligation at once to choose life, he insisted on instant, decisive, and visible action!

His singleness of aim begat simplicity of matter and manner. His words did not hide his thought and his illustrations did not call attention to themselves. They were windows to let in light, and the elaborate framework and stained glass that adorn the window, make the light dim. He dared not interpose his greatness between dying souls and the cross, and desired to be nothing but the finger, pointing, and the voice saying, "Behold the Lamb of God!"

His obvious sincerity impressed his hearers with the conviction that he believed and knew what he said. He bade his pupils preach only what was bathed in their own rich, personal experience. "Sensational" sermons were, to him, awful trifling, poulticing [Editor's Note: Polticing is treating a wound with a substance that draws the infection out.] the deadly cancer that is eating at the vitals and calls, at once, for the knife! This intense sincerity lent authority and majesty to his searching exposures of deceptive experiences and false hopes. Among these are Ritualism which has the form, without the power, of godliness, or Pharisaism which lacks the spirit and motive of a holy morality, or upon the dead past which is contradicted by the living present. It fitted him to rebuke the dishonest toward God, which appears even in self-examination and in prayer, asking for what we neither expect nor will to receive, and in habitual disregard of the voice of conscience and of the Spirit.

His preaching was Scriptural. The Bible was his constant and devout study, with the arrangement and adaptation of its truths to human souls. It was the armory where he found weapons, defensive and offensive, and took unto him the panoply of God. It was the treasure, whence, as a householder, he brought forth things new and old.

He preached the whole Gospel. The Law, with its stern demand and perfect standard, he used as a plough to sweep away refuges of lies and tear up false hopes by the roots. Then he followed it with the love of God, as the sower gently drops into the furrow the seed steeped in his tears. The sword of the Spirit is two-edged. Warning, or invitation, alone, like a scimitar, may strike effective blows in one direction; but when the two keen edges meet in the point, they prepare us for the thrust that pierces to the joints and marrow.

Thus Mr. Finney begat deep conviction of sin. As Socrates sought to lead men "from ignorance unconscious to ignorance conscious," he aimed to produce that consciousness of guilt and peril without which there can be no deep sense of need or of obligation.

How spiritual, too, was the tone of his preaching! With what ardor and fervor he besought men to be justified and sanctified by faith. With what burning, glowing zeal, did he assail the sectarianism that cares for sect more than for Christ and the conventionalism whose "awful respectability" hampers ministers and churches by a false fastidiousness, and dares not break through the bonds of custom, and adopt a new measure, even to save a soul! With what scathing rebuke he exposes the idle neglect that leaves generations to die without the Gospel, though for each disciple to win one soul each year to Christ, would be to covert the world within the lifetime of a single generation!

His preaching was spiritual in power as well as tone. He depended on the Spirit, whose blessed unction alone fits us to plead with men, or even to understand the Gospel. With the agony of Jacob at Jabbok, he sought the power to witness. "Honour the Holy Spirit and He will honour you," was his maxim; and he taught that without the habitual recognition of dependence on the Spirit, revivals neither begin nor continue.

If any one secret of Mr. Finney's power be emphatic, it is this: he gave his whole soul to God.

There is a Scottish legend for whose historic verity we do not vouch, that when Bruce, the Deliverer of Scotland, died, Douglas carried his heart, embalmed, into his battles with Edward IV. In the heat of the fight, he would fling the heart toward the enemy's lines and shout, "Forth, heart of Bruce, and Douglas will follow or die!" Charles G. Finney flung his own heart forward to the feet of God; over and across this world, with its hollow treasures and shallow pleasures, into the spiritual and eternal! Then he followed his heart, until, as a redeemed and perfected saint, he reached the goal where his affections had long been lodged!

Give yourself, with such sublime simplicity of aim, to God and His service; empty yourself as completely of worldly and selfish ambition; seek as devoutly to be filled and moved by the Spirit; and God will be as willing to use you as a chosen vessel for His glory!

2

DELIGHTING IN THE LORD

From: The Oberlin Evangelist
July 2, 1845

> *"Delight thyself also in the Lord; and He shall give thee the desires of thine heart"*
>
> —Psalm 37:4

In speaking from these words I shall,

I. Show what is implied in delighting ourselves in the Lord.

II. Show what is implied in the promise, "He shall give thee the desires of thine heart."

III. Show why this promise is so conditioned.

I. WHAT IS IMPLIED IN DELIGHTING OURSELVES IN THE LORD.

1. Absolute sympathy with Him. No one can really delight himself in the Lord any more than he sympathizes with God in respect to the great end on which God's heart is set, and the means by which He is attempting to accomplish that end. He must adopt God's principles and enter into His views and feelings. He must respond with a hearty amen to God's character, works, ways, all the truths of His word, and all the dispensations of His providence. One who has this absolute sympathy with God, and who deeply interests himself in God's character, government, policy, ends and means, will of course delight himself in the Lord; and no one else will.

2. Delighting ourselves in the Lord implies a supreme complacency in Him. Complacency in God is benevolence or good will toward God, modified by a consideration of His character and relations. This always implies delight.

[Editors note: The word complacency in modern usage frequently has a more negative sense of meaning and typically denotes smugness or an attitude lacking motivation regardless of importance, danger, trouble or controversy. The way Charles Finney uses the word, however, carries a very positive sense. The meaning he is communicating is "the fact or state of being pleased with a person or thing." So, then, complacency in the Lord denotes pleasure, satisfaction and delight in Him.]

Complacency is often spoken of as if it consisted completely in a delight existing in the sensibility of the soul. However, properly speaking this is not so. Complacency considered as a virtue, belongs to the will or heart. Nevertheless, it always implies a corresponding state of sensibility; and of course, implies a delight or pleasure in view of the character, government, relations, works, and ways of God. Without this complacency of heart in God, we cannot be said truly to delight ourselves in Him.

3. Delight in the Lord implies that He is chosen as the

supreme good of the soul. The text undoubtedly implies this. It is setting our supreme affections on Him, and choosing Him as our all-satisfying portion, making Him the great center in which the affections and sympathy of our soul delight to rest.

4. Delight in God implies universal confidence in Him. We could never be said truly to delight ourselves in God, unless we had supreme, universal confidence in His character, providence, and word. We could not choose anything as an all-satisfying portion, unless the mind regarded it as infinite and perfect. The mind is so composed that it cannot be satisfied with any thing else.

The mind is dissatisfied naturally and necessarily with whatever is perceived as imperfect. Delight in God implies that the mind regards Him as possessing infinite fullness, perfection, and truthfulness, and every attribute that can fill and satisfy the soul. It is common for men to seek for what they suppose will make them happy, and to endeavor to find happiness in the creature.

However, nothing but the infinitely perfect Creator can satisfy the wants and demands of the soul. Therefore, to delight ourselves in the Lord, in the sense of the text, implies that we are satisfied in God and that His fullness and perfection meet all the demands of our being. In addition, it means that in Him we have enough; and that the mind regards Him as an exceeding great reward, a portion infinitely ample, satisfying, full and overflowing, infinitely glorious and eternal.

5. Delight in God implies universal submission of our will to His. The soul that is not entirely submissive to God, cannot be delighted in Him. This person is like a child whose will is not submissive to the will of his parent. He becomes restless under the divine government, often made unhappy by the dispensations of His providence and by the requirements of His Word.

To have true delight in God implies that we have no will of our own—only that the will of God should be done. It implies that the soul has come practically to regard God as infinitely wise and good, to feel the fullest satisfaction with His appointments and His dispensations whatever they may be.

6. Delight in God implies a spirit of universal obedience to Him. This obedience creates a state of mind that inquires after what God would have us do with a fixed intention to do all His will without hesitation and to devote ourselves entirely to pleasing Him. It implies in short, that our whole being is given up to it; that we have no purpose or design, but in all things, at all times, in all places, and forever, to live wholly to Him.

7. Delight in God implies delight in obeying Him, or delight in His service. It is one thing to obey, and another thing to have delight in obedience. To be sure, our nature is such that true obedience always produces delight. However, obedience and delight are not the same things. Where the true spirit of obedience exists, we shall find our delight and happiness of course in the service of God. We are always delighted with the course on which our heart is supremely set.

Our hearts, therefore, must be given up to pleasing God and living to this end. When we are consecrated to God's glory and interests, heartily and universally, nothing will afford us so great a pleasure and delight as waiting on God, doing His bidding, and in every thing engaged in His service. The service of God will be our meat and drink. We shall know what Christ meant when He said, "I have meat to eat that ye know not of." "It is my meat to do the will of him that sent me." "I delight to do thy will, O my God."

8. Delight in God implies a deep interest in His honour and glory. Everything we do and say will have reference to God. God will be the supreme end of all we say and do. In this, we shall sympathize with God Himself. God has a supreme regard to His own interest and glory, and is the chief end of all His works.

This is by no means selfishness in God. It is not because it is His own glory, but because it is infinitely the greatest good, that He has a supreme regard for it. God's well being is of infinitely more value than the total of the well-being of all creatures that ever were or could be made. God's well-being is infinite whereas the well-being of all creatures will always be finite. Nothing can be infinite that is not eternally and necessarily so. Nothing finite can ever grow and increase until it becomes infinite. Therefore the total well-being of all finite creatures must always be finite and of course infinitely less than the well-being of God.

Now if God would regard things according to their relative value He must necessarily lay infinitely more stress upon His own happiness and glory than upon the happiness and glory of all other beings together. There is no comparison between the finite and the infinite, and therefore the total value of the endless happiness of all creatures is absolutely as nothing when put into the scale against the well-being of God.

God so regards this, and it is reasonable, right, and infinitely important that He should. Consequently Himself, His own glory, and His well-being, are the supreme end of all His works. When I saw this truth taught in Pres. Edwards' writings many years ago, I did not immediately perceive its truthfulness. Moreover, I have often since heard persons speak as if they were offended by such a teaching as if it implied selfishness in God.

Selfishness is preferring our own interests to our neighbors, simply because it is our own. It is not selfish in us to prefer our happiness to the happiness of a goose, because ours is more valuable. However, it is selfish in us to prefer our happiness to our neighbor's, when his is equally valuable with our own.

I repeat it again; it is not because the happiness or glory is God's that His heart is set supremely on it, but because of its intrinsic value, because it is so infinitely the greater good. Now delight in God implies that we regard this as He does, as far as we understand it. It also implies that we sympathize with Him in this; that we regard His interests as the supreme and infinite good, and delight ourselves in promoting His glory and honour in the universe; that we find our supreme happiness and satisfaction of soul in this.

9. Delight in God implies that we supremely seek and desire eternal union and communion with Him and that as far as our own happiness is concerned, this is all we ask. Give us this and we could lack nothing essential to our happiness; but deprive us of this, and nothing in the universe could satisfy us - to have eternal union and communion with the ever blessed God.

II. WHAT IS IMPLIED IN THE PROMISE

The promise, "Delight thyself in the Lord, and He shall give thee the desires of thine heart," implies that we shall have those things on which we set our affections, or in other words that our desire, our really cherished desires, shall be gratified. If we delight ourselves in the Lord, we shall have all things on which we set our hearts. "He shall give thee the desires of thine heart"—there is no limit, in fact, plainly implied is that what we set our hearts on, and that which we pray for shall be granted.

It seems to me that the text is to be understood, not that every transient desire or awaking of appetite shall be gratified, but that the supreme desire of the soul, that on which we can properly be said to fix our affections and our heart shall infallibly be granted to us.

III. WHY THIS PROMISE IS THUS CONDITIONED.

1. Because without this condition the promise would be unsafe to the universe. For God to promise unqualifiedly to give us the desire of our heart, unless He knew that we had a complete sympathy with Him, would be unreasonable, unsafe, and something He could not innocently do. What would it amount to for Him to make such a promise without this condition? It would amount to our selfish desires being granted.

However, when selfishness is slain, when our supreme desire is on God, and our whole soul sympathizes deeply with Him, it is plain that our desires may be granted. It is then both consistent with the will of God, and with the highest good of being to grant our desires. God is then the great end and center of the desires of the soul, and in giving Himself to the soul He gratifies its desires.

2. God could not safely make such a promise except on this condition because it would be impossible to fulfill it. Suppose He should make the unqualified promise to every individual that He should have the desires of his heart. With the endless lustings of men after objects around them, how often would it happen that different persons would desire the same things when only one could possess them?

3. It is perfectly safe for God to make such a promise on the condition of delighting ourselves in the Lord, because whosoever delights himself in the Lord can never desire anything inconsistent with the will of God. The Spirit of God dwells in him; all his affections and desires are under the influence of the Spirit of God. In addition, while he delights himself in God, he is sure not to set his heart on anything unless the Spirit of God draws him to it. In this case, certainly he cannot at the same time be lusting after a forbidden object and delighting himself in the Lord.

4. This promise is thus conditioned because God delights to bestow that desire on which the heart is set that delights in Him. He loves to bestow Himself, to communicate of His own fullness to those who set their hearts on Him. He loves those that love Him.

There is a sense to be sure in which God loves His enemies; but His love to them is not a delight in their persons or characters. However, He greatly enjoys the communication of Himself to those who delight themselves in Him. He loves to draw them into a participation of His joy that they may drink of the river of His pleasure. He delights in making them partakers of His own divine nature, of His own holiness and of His own happiness.

5. It is of the highest importance to the universe that God should grant the desires of the heart that delights itself in Him. It is for the highest good of being that He should do so. It is for His glory; it contributes to the stability of His government. It is not only highly honourable to God, but also highly useful to His creatures to know that God will grant the desire of those who set their heart on Him.

REMARKS

1. Those that delight themselves in God will of course manifest great cheerfulness of mind.

... because this delight in God is of itself a cheerful state of mind, and

... because they have the desires of the heart.

An unsatisfied craving of mind, that produces unhappiness, gloom, despondency, and despair, is not the portion of the mind that delights itself in God. The soul that delights itself in God is pleased with whatever happens. It has no way or will of its own, and therefore cannot be disappointed. It has no craving or lusting of a selfish nature, and therefore is not disappointed by being crossed and denied things on which its affections are set, because its affections are set on nothing but God. While it delights itself in God it is of course cheerful and happy under all circumstances, and can rejoice evermore, and pray without ceasing, and in every thing give thanks.

2. From what has been said, we may see why so few prayers prevail with God. The fact is, there is so much dissatisfaction with God and so much lusting after other things, that God cannot fulfill the desires of such souls; it would be infinitely unwise and unsafe to do so. Then, as a condition of prevailing prayer, we must delight ourselves in the Lord, and when we do this our prayers will be dictated by God's Spirit, and of course will be answered.

Now look around over the world. How few seem to have their supreme delight in God. How few are seeking communion and fellowship with God. How few make union with God the supreme end of their lives. It is not strange then that our prayers are not answered. The conditions of prevailing prayer are not fulfilled.

Many pray because they are pressed up to it by conviction, not because their soul pants after communion with God, and delights itself in God. Instead of loving to dwell in the Bible, and in the house of God, and in the closet—in short, instead of delighting itself in God, it is constantly roving about here and there, to see if it cannot find some good. "Who will show us any good?" seems to be its constant inquiry. Now those who are in this state cannot have their desires granted.

The reason why so many desires are ungratified is that they are not the right kind of desires. The truth is, where an individual delights himself in the Lord, he will have the desires of his heart.

Instead of being wretched all the time, and setting his heart on some thing he cannot get, when he comes to delight himself in the Lord, all this scrambling and lusting after what is beyond his reach, will be gone; he will be like a weaned child, all peace. When the mind has God, it has enough.

Much prayer, or that which is called prayer, is after all, nothing but lusting in the Bible sense of the term. It is a craving of the mind after some selfish good. Much prayer is nothing else but the pouring out of these cravings of the selfish heart. The Apostle James speaks of this state of mind; "Ye lust, says he, and have not; ye kill and desire to have, and cannot obtain; ye fight and war, yet ye have not because ye ask not; ye ask and receive not because ye ask amiss, that ye may consume it on your lusts."

3. When there is delight in God, the supreme desire of course, will be for union and communion with God. This will be the all-absorbing desire of the mind. It will swallow up all other desires. I will explain a little.

We often see one state of mind or desire that comes to swallow up all others. The mind becomes so engrossed with one object of desire as to care for little else besides. We see this state of mind often in this world. One desire seems to eat up and swallow up all the rest. We see this too sometimes in the case of individuals that are very wicked. The drunkard's appetite for strong drink sometimes, will kill and completely destroy every other appetite; even natural affection seems to be annihilated by it.

Sometimes a husband's affection for his wife is so strong, that he cares for almost nothing else. If the object of his affection is lost, he says, "What have I more? I have nothing to care for now." His interest in every thing else is destroyed.

Now let this illustrate what I mean here. When the mind

becomes acquainted with God and the sensibility is rightly developed toward Him, as it always must be before it can be at rest, and all the desires center in God, he comes to be the supreme end of the soul in such a sense. Now take anything away that you will, and leave his God, and you cannot affect his happiness; this one desire so swallows up all the rest.

With such a soul, nothing else weighs a straw in comparison to the love of God. Christ was so swallowed up at one time with this one great idea, that when it was told Him saying, "Behold thy mother and thy brethren stand without desiring to speak with thee;" He replied, "Who is my mother? and who are by brethren? And he stretched forth his hand toward his disciples and said, Behold my mother and my brethren. For whosoever shall do the will of my Father which is in Heaven, the same is my mother, and sister and brother." He meant to rebuke the idea that our blood relatives are to be considered so much dearer than our spiritual relatives.

He would say to those who sustain this relation to God, "Ye are my mother and my brethren." Now whoever has His sensibility much developed toward God, comes to feel that every thing must sustain some relation to this end, or it is of no value. Nothing else pleases. It must bear a relation to God, to His government, and to His glory, to make it of any regard to such a mind.

The thing nearest and dearest to people naturally, if it does not sustain this relation, will be cast off as of no value. Some time ago, one person said to another, "I am praying that the Lord would destroy your influence." "Well," remarked the other, "I hope the Lord will answer your prayers if my influence is not good, because it is of no use to me unless it can glorify God, and if it does no good, I hope it will be destroyed."

Now I suppose that individual answered just as he felt. He felt that his influence was worth nothing. Unless it would do some good to the universe, he cared nothing about it. Now when an individual comes into this state of mind, he regards everything in this light. He must be valuable to God or he cares nothing about it.

We oftentimes see persons so much attached to others in this world as to seem really to enjoy nothing only as it sustains some relation to the object of their affection. Husbands and wives sometimes sustain this relation so that every thing is valued or not valued according to the relation it sustains to the one or the other. Now I suppose the mind becomes so completely swallowed up in God, so "sick in love," and so ravished with the love of God, and comes to take such delight in Him as to say with the Psalmist, "Whom have I in heaven but thee, O God."

The Psalmist knew what he said, "Whom have I in heaven but thee!" His father and mother, and many whom he had greatly loved, had gone to heaven, but still he exclaims, "Whom have I in heaven but thee?" His children, and those to whom he was greatly attached, were all around him, and yet when he comes to think of God, his whole soul cries out, "There is none upon earth that I desire besides thee."

This will be the case with a mind ravished and carried away with the love of God in this way. There is a dying of the mind to all other things including self, the world, friends, and everything, so that the individual comes to care for nothing, not even to take his food, unless for the glory of God. He is dead to all but God. How safe it is, then, for God, to make such a promise as this, to an individual who thus delights himself in God!

4. An individual who delights himself in the Lord will postpone everything that comes in competition with communion with God. You will not find him making excuses for not attending prayer meetings, for not spending time in his closet, and holding much communion with God. You see, persons who seem to be really honest in saying they would like to commune with God or attend the prayer meeting, but they have worked very hard to day, or they have so much to do, or there is some good excuse, and they cannot attend. Now I have learned that when persons come to really delight themselves in the Lord, that such excuses do not appear to be really important.

Show me a man whose soul is panting after God, who can say with the Psalmist, "As the hart panteth after the water-brook, so panteth my soul after thee, O God." Such a man will love to go where he can have communion with God. He will as naturally postpone every thing else that interferes with his communion with God, as he draws his breath. The truth is, when persons make such excuses about reading their Bible and attending meetings, the secret is, they have lost their keen relish for communion with God, and are beginning to lose their delight in Him.

5. If we delight ourselves in God, He will delight Himself in us; and He will delight Himself in us just in proportion as we delight ourselves in Him. As we seek communion with Him, so will He seek communion with us. God loves society—the society of the holy. If we embrace Him, He will embrace us. If we pant after Him, He will pant after us. If we are drawn to Him, He will be drawn to us. This is a law of mind. It is impossible that He should not delight in the soul that delights in Him; impossible that He should not seek after the soul that seeks after Him.

It would be the same thing as denying Himself, to not delight in those that delight in Him. Whenever a mind seeks union with God, God sets His heart on that soul. It is as dear to Him as the apple of His eye. He loves it as He loves His own soul. Why should He not? It is like Him; it is a part of Him; it is so to speak, flesh of His flesh, and bone of His bone. It has come to assimilate to His own nature. He comes to love it as He loves the man Christ Jesus, and for the same reason. Moreover, He will no more turn from it and not hear it than He would turn from His own beloved Son, Jesus Christ.

Now we ought to understand this, that whenever we find ourselves strongly drawn to God, God is infinitely drawn toward us; when our heart is panting after God, he is panting after us. More! It is God panting after us that draws us toward Him! This should be understood. It is of great importance that we should get this thing fixed in our mind, that when our mind is tending toward God, He is tending toward us. "Draw nigh to me," says God, "and I will draw nigh to you, Turn unto me, and I will turn unto you." Love me, and I will love you.

6. The soul that delights in God, will greatly mourn, if for any reason, communion is withheld. Those will be days of mourning to that soul, when, for any reason God withholds the light of His countenance. It is impossible for Him, then, to be cheerful and happy. He may have confidence, and say with David, "Why art thou cast down, O my soul? and why art thou disquieted within me? Hope thou in God; for I shall yet praise Him, who is the health of my countenance, and my God." Now in this case the Psalmist had confidence in God, but he mourned. In such a case, the soul is ready to cry out, "My God, my God, why hast thou forsaken me?"

I have thought many times that there was not so much mystery in what Christ said, at the time, as many would make us believe. The Christian, that knows what it is to commune and walk with God, and to have God withdraw His countenance from him, will naturally use this same language. He will cry out with the Psalmist, "Will the Lord cast off forever? Will He be favorable no more? Is His mercy clean gone forever? Doth His promise fail forever more? Hath God forgotten to be gracious? Hath He in anger shut up His tender mercies?" It is not strange that Christ should cry out, as He did. God's countenance was withdrawn from Him, and He could not help crying out to God to know why this was so.

Where an individual has come to delight himself in God, and falls into this state of mind in which he mourns, his mourning will be very submissive and very peculiar. It will be nothing like the mourning of this world. Not a rebellious, complaining state of mind. It will be the mourning of a "weaned child," very submissive—a peculiar kind of mourning, and a peculiar kind of submission. It is not rebellious or complaining, and yet it is not joyful. It is not distrustful. "Hope thou in God" is its language, "for I shall yet praise Him." It expects good from God. "I shall rejoice! Yes, for my Father will not always hide His face from me."

When these seasons last long they lead the soul into such a state of showing the individual to himself, that he is filled with a deep grief. This will bring him to utter unearthly, heart-rending groans, and an expression of holy submission in a child-like dependence on God and confidence and hope in Him. Oh if the sinner could only hear him and listen to such an individual when he supposed none but God near, he would go away and say, "Now I know, as I exist, I know there is such a thing as communion with God. O such expressions! such language! I know God was there!"

When I was an impenitent sinner, I had been out to attend to some law business. Returning and passing by a schoolhouse, I heard a man praying. That prayer did more to impress my mind with the subject of religion, than all I had heard before, from my birth. I have not the least doubt but that such a prayer would affect almost any man of reflection, could he hear it.

The man did not know that any one could hear him. He had left his work in the field, and had retired to the schoolhouse for secret communion with God. As I rode along, I heard him and stopped, and listened to what he said. Oh! It set my mind on fire! That was what I had never witnessed before; it seemed as if I was brought right into the presence of God!

The very tones of his voice, before I could understand what he said, seemed to come down upon me, like the voice of God from heaven. Every word he spoke seemed to come right from the bottom of his heart. His voice was frequently choked with groans, and sighs. It was the voice of a man pleading with God!

When an individual is in this state of mind I am speaking of, when he has fallen into darkness from any reason whatever, although he mourns, he will not betake himself to any other source of happiness. He has gone too far in this way, to go anywhere else for happiness.

When a person has but little grace, he will sometimes betake himself to other objects, run into company, and go here and there, trying this thing and that, to get happiness. However, when one has come to delight himself in God, and the supreme desire of his soul has centered in God—now let him fall into such circumstances as I have mentioned, and he will not betake himself to such and such places and scenes, to make himself happy!

No. Indeed, he will not. He will say, "O God, I cannot, I will not go anywhere else for happiness. O God, thou hast taught me to love thee; thou hast weaned my soul from everything else, so that I cannot love anything but thee, and now, wilt thou take thyself, thou who are my all, from me? O my God, I will find my joy in thee, or joy I will never have." Such will be the language of a soul in this state.

Hearer, do you know what this is. You will know if you will give yourself up to God, so as to be all absorbed in Him, so that your whole being will be given up to God. If this is not the case with you, you need to be crucified.

7. The happiness that the soul, that delights itself in God, finds in Him, is so different from all other delight, so peculiar, it is like no other happiness in the world. All other joy is nothing at all like it. It has such a peculiarity, such purity—there is nothing that can compare with it. The intelligence, the heart, the sensibility, the whole being is so satisfied in God. Oh! I wish I had some unspeakable word to express this!

For we need some unearthly language to express what every Christian has, when he comes into such a state of mind with God. He is so elevated in God. He is drinking the very river of which God drinks. There is such a peculiarity, such sweetness in this, that the soul abhors all other joy. It cannot go and sip, and sip, in the polluted fountains of this world. What are they! What are they? Shall a man, who has bathed in the very atmosphere of heaven—shall he go about to sip of the filthy cups of this world? Never! Never! Only as he delights in God can he find any delight whatever. He cares for nothing else but what comes from God.

8. Be sure when you pray, that you fulfill these conditions, that you delight yourself in God.

9. He that will be content with God, and will really be satisfied with God, may have as much of God as he will. In addition, just in proportion, as we give ourselves up to find our delight in God, just in that proportion shall we have delight in God. Go the universe over, and you will find, just in proportion as the soul gives itself up to God, just in that proportion, it finds its fullness in God.

If you divide your enjoyment, how can God fill your cup? Just empty your whole heart of self and of everything else, then hold it up to God, and He will fill it with His own purity, with His own love and blessedness. Yes, you will have it filled with the ocean of God.

3

THE JOY OF GOD'S SALVATION

April 13, 1849

"Restore unto me the joy of thy salvation!"
—Psalm 51:12

In speaking from these words, I shall,

1. Show what the Psalmist prayed for.

2. Why he prayed for it.

3. The essential elements of such a prayer.

4. What is implied in offering such a prayer acceptably.

THE ELEMENTS THAT ENTER INTO THE JOY OF GOD'S SALVATION

It is significant to observe here that there are elements in this joy that do not belong to the holy joy of beings who have never sinned. The saved sinner has some forms of joy that the unfallen angel has not and can not have. From this, I do not infer that the sinful, when saved, are happier than the sinless who have never needed salvation. I only say that the joy of each has elements in it that are unlike those of the other. This must be seen by everyone who enters at all into the peculiar circumstances and state of mind of each class.

The words of our text are found in what is called David's penitential psalm. This psalm, as the caption states and as the scope sufficiently shows, was written with reference to David's great sin in the matter of Bathsheba and Uriah. It may have been written at the very time of his being rebuked by Nathan and of his becoming penitent. However, if written sometime, more or less, afterwards, it was evidently in recollection of those events, so that we must regard these circumstances as being the occasion of the prayer in our text.

WHAT ARE THE PRINCIPLE INGREDIENTS OR ELEMENTS OF THIS STATE OF MIND?

1. A sense of pardon. A man might repent, and yet not have in full measure the joys of God's salvation because one element of this joy is a sense of pardon. The sinner needs to have the revelation made to him that God forgives him.

2. A sense of divine reconciliation. We can consider that a man may be truly penitent and yet have no manifestations made to his soul of God's forgiving grace. He might not see that God is reconciled to him. He might not think of or believe any such thing. Nevertheless, in the case of a sinner convicted of sin, it is plain that some degree of divine manifestations on this point is essential to constitute the joy of God's salvation. It might not be essential to a sinless being; but must be to one who like David has sinned, and feels himself to have fallen under the divine displeasure.

3. The love of complacency. The Scriptures speak of "the love of God shed abroad in the heart by the Holy Ghost." The experience of Christians show that this shedding abroad of divine love in the heart by the Holy Ghost usually follows the deep experiences of penitence and of faith in redeeming blood.

This love of complacency is a state of the deep feelings as opposed to any action of the will. It consists substantially in emotions of pleasure and delight in God and in His ways and works, and differs essentially from the love of benevolence. It is one of the elements of a forgiven sinner's joy.

4. A sense of inward purity. I do not suppose an individual could have the joy of God's salvation unless he had a sense of inward purity. He could not have real and rich joy unless he felt as Brainard expressed himself, "I am clean from both past and present sin."

Without this element, one may have excitement, but cannot have the real joy of God's salvation because he still lacks the real salvation itself. He still lacks that in which the real blessedness of a saved soul chiefly consists, namely, inward purity and positive deliverance from present sin. When God applies the energy of His Spirit to renew the soul, and in place of selfish lusts, to shed abroad His own love in the heart, there is begotten a sweet sense of present purity. In addition, the soul has the witness in itself that sin is put away, and that divine love has taken its place.

5. A sense of inward harmony. By this, I refer to a state of mind that is in harmony with God, itself, and all other holy beings in the universe. Its own powers are brought into such fitting correlation with each other, and all together are in such relations to God, that the very working of their perfect machinery produces harmony. Perhaps there is no word that expresses this delightful result as well as the word, harmony. It is indeed like the harmony of sweet music. Each separate vibration fits every other, and together they produce the results of most exquisite harmony. None will understand this unless they have a keen comprehension of what the word harmony means.

I have often been struck to see how differently men will understand the meaning of words, or language. It is so with regard to this word, harmony. Some minds have no just conception of what harmony is. However, one who has a keen relish for harmony in sounds, who has a cultivated taste, and an ear well attuned, can understand what is intended by harmony of soul when all its powers are in tune.

He can also understand it by the law of contrast. Let him listen to the grating discord of a piano or worse still of an organ when utterly out of tune. Oh, how it rakes His sensibilities! In the same way, the mind in its unconverted state is out of tune. It passes along slowly in its progress toward becoming attuned to the sweet harmony of love.

However, when God Himself sits down to put it in tune; when He really takes it in hand and puts every pipe and every string in order, so that He can run His divine fingers over it, and make it breathe forth the very harmony of heaven, then, Oh what music! No words can describe it! Nevertheless, if you will commit your own soul into God's hands, that He may put it in spiritual tune, you may learn by experience what it is. You will find it a most blessed experience.

When every power, affection, and element of your soul's activities is in such tune that not a note, not even a semitone can be found in it which is not perfectly in tune, then what rich harmony will it discourse! Peace will be an all-pervading element in the atmosphere of your soul. Every opinion, every emotion, every affection is in harmony with God.

6. Of course there will be implied in this, a delight in the whole revealed will of God; in all His character; in all He does and in all He omits to do. It involves acquiescence to all His providential arrangements, including all He accomplishes and all He neglect to accomplish. When this state of mind exists in its purity, there is a universal satisfaction of mind in God. Every want and demand both of our nature and of our circumstances is seen to be perfectly met in God. A deep comprehension of this forms a prominent part of the joy of God's salvation.

WHY SHOULD THIS BLESSING BE SOUGHT IN PRAYER?

1. The thing is desirable in itself. It is in itself a good, and therefore it is lawful to pray for it.

2. It is honourable to God that His people should possess this joy. Such happiness ought to characterize the children of so great and so bountiful a Father.

3. Its absence is greatly dishonourable to God. Is it not dishonourable to a king that His "children should go mourning all their days?" How strange that those who profess to be children of God should have no joy! What! Is it not dishonourable to God to have His people lean and ill-favored, going about the streets like walking skeletons? As if He could endure this Himself; and not only so, but even like them the better for their rags and filthiness! Who can believe this? What prince on earth ever kept His court and above all, His children, looking in such style?

4. It is not only dishonourable to God, but highly disgraceful for Christians to live without spiritual joy and peace. Consider what is implied in a Christian's complaining of the absence of spiritual joy. It must imply either that God is very careful about giving His children occasions of joy, or that they are loath to embrace and improve those occasions.

5. The joy of the Christian is exceedingly useful to others. Who can estimate the value of a living fountain of water in a barren desert? Like Siloam's well in a land of drought or like an oasis in a wilderness is a Christian who has always something to say of the joy of God's salvation. His words and his spirit are all the more reviving because so many are always complaining. How often are we grieved and distressed with these complaints!

On the other hand, a single joyous-hearted Christian is a priceless blessing in a family. To have one such Christian in each household who should be so full of the joys of God's salvation that he could not help speaking it out on all fit occasions would be like planting a well-spring of water in every acre of earth's desert sands. How soon would the wilderness rejoice and blossom as the rose! How often has one such Christian set a whole community on fire with desire to get rid of their darkness and come forth into God's glorious light!

6. The spiritual joy of Christians is exceedingly useful to sinners. Sinners know that Christians ought to rejoice in God, and of course, they are not surprised at all that they should. How impressive to the sinner to see that the Christian is at rest in God! Oh, he knows nothing of that peace himself; and the view of it as enjoyed by the Christian reveals his own desolation.

What sinner was ever in the habit of mingling in the society of Christians whose heart and lips are full of joy, without feeling unutterable yearnings of heart for such joys as these? I can well recollect that some of my earliest impressions of a serious nature were occasioned by hearing a young man speak of his joy in God. I went home from that meeting weeping. I said to myself, "That joy is rations. It is a joy worthy of a human soul."

I walked along with many tears, and when alone, I sought a retired and dry place to kneel down and pray that God would give me what that young man had. None that I had ever heard of sermons and lectures had made half so much impression as that young man's religious joy.

Sinners know that their own joy is a mean affair. Hence, when they see the Christian's joy, they cannot help contrasting it with their own, and the result can scarcely fail of revealing to them their own wretched state. These struggles of the sinner for joy are indeed altogether selfish.

My prayers at the time I just mentioned were selfish in this way. Nevertheless, they were useful, because they served to enforce conviction of the value of religion and of the worthlessness of everything short of it. The Psalmist understood the value of Christian joy. "Restore unto me," said he, "the joy of they salvation; then will I teach transgressors thy ways, and sinners shall be converted unto thee." He knew this would make a powerful impression on their minds, for good.

7. The absence of this spiritual joy is a great stumbling block to all classes. What a stumbling block to a church to have a minister who is perpetually in spiritual darkness and trouble! How can he lead on the sacramental host whose own heart is shrinking back with spiritual fears, or suffering under spiritual agonies himself!

Moreover, the more important the position a man holds, the more desirable it becomes that he should be full of the joy and peace which the Holy Ghost inspires. Whether deacons in a church, parents in a family, or professors in a college, how can men who hold such stations of responsibility ever think of acquitting themselves of their responsibilities without possessing grace enough to give them the joy of God's salvation?

In saying this I would not be understood to imply that Christians never have trials and sorrows. They will doubtlessly have them, but even in these very trials and sorrows, how precious will be the joys of God's salvation to their souls!

This joy of God's salvation is especially indispensable to one who preaches the gospel! A man might preach something without this joy, but not the gospel. He might deliver moral essays or might contend valiantly for his polemic creed. However, as for preaching the vital matters of salvation, how can he if he knows nothing about them by experience? He needs such faith as brings peace; such communion of soul with God as necessarily brings joy of heart.

This is something more than being penitent and of course something more than being merely pious. The Psalmist knew that he was penitent, and yet he also knew that he needed something more. God had not yet revealed the light of His own face. That is why, when he had confessed and humbled himself before God, it remained that he should pray, "Restore unto me the joy of thy salvation."

David had known well what it was to be full of joy before God. He had danced for joy with all his might before the ark of the Lord, and often we find him preparing songs of joy and praise. But now, alas, his harp is silent and all unstrung! He has sinned grievously against God. A thick cloud has come over his soul, and though he has confessed, yet still he has occasion to pray, "Restore unto me the joy of thy salvation."

Why does he want these joys? Without them he cannot reach transgressors for any good purpose. What Christian does not know how to sympathize with David in this state of mind? Who has not known experientially the state of those who have sinned, confessed, but still have the greatest occasion to ask God to restore to them the lost joys of His salvation? The soul cries out, "Lord, how can I live, shut out in darkness from thee? O, if thou canst, wilt thou not reveal thy reconciled face and restore again those lost joys of thy salvation?"

THE CONDITIONS UPON WHICH THIS PRAYER CAN BE ANSWERED

1. We must have a sense of our own sins, and their deep and damning guilt. I said that some of the elements in the Christian's joy do not exist in the joy of sinless beings in the universe of God. In the Christian's case, it is indispensable that his joy should be preceded by a sense of sin and guilt. Otherwise he cannot appreciate the grace of pardon or, in fact, anything about the gospel. He needs such a sense of sin as to understand how great a thing it is to be delivered from sin, rescued from its farther commission, and pardoned of its horrible guilt.

2. Confession of sin, and real repentance. God would be but poorly employed in restoring the joys of salvation to one who has not repented.

3. Making restitution also must be a condition, for this is essential to real repentance.

4. A comprehension of the atonement and way of acceptance. I have said that one might repent and yet not have this sense of restored joy. I know this to be the case and I believe every

Christian in this house knows it. In order to have this joy, we need a sense of pardon, but this is not all.

We need the kind of sense of pardon and a view of its mode that justifies God. We need such a view as will show that God is just in pardoning the sinner. The sinner in the appropriate state of mind is not selfish, therefore he desires God to be justified, and could not be happy to receive pardon in any way which he did not see would fully acquit and greatly glorify God.

He needs to see that the gospel mode of pardon is such as most fully justifies and honours God. He needs to see that the atonement through Jesus Christ most perfectly answers all these great and most desirable ends. I do not believe it possible for a man to enter into the joys of God's salvation without some just notions of the atonement as the way in which God can be glorious in forgiving sin.

5. Another essential condition is the acceptance of Christ in the fullness of His relations. Unless we see what relations Christ sustains to us, and what He consequently can do for us, it is impossible that we can experience this joy. Unless we apprehend Christ's fullness, we cannot receive fully the joys of His salvation.

Another condition is universal confidence in God. If there be any one thing in which we do not have confidence in God, there will be chafing and trouble. The soul is not right toward God.

Again, an entire renunciation of self is a condition. Whoever does not renounce himself, cannot have this joy.

You must renounce all idols. What would you think of God if He were to give this joy to those who are sipping at every fountain of earthly pleasure, trying to find some little joy besides that from God?

There must also be sympathy of will with God. Our will must be so thoroughly with His that we can go with Him in all He does, without the least reluctance or misgiving.

Again, subdued appetites and passions are essential, for while these are clamoring for indulgence, it is utterly impossible for the soul to experience the joys of God's salvation.

Another condition is the indwelling Spirit of God because who will have his appetites subdued, or indeed, who will fulfill any of these conditions without the Spirit?

It is essential that there should be a clear medium of communication between our souls and God. A man who does not have communion with God cannot have the joys of gospel salvation. When for any reason, the soul is shut out from God and the communion is not free, but God hides His face, then the soul cannot rejoice in the joy of His great salvation.

WHAT IS IMPLIED IN OFFERING SUCH A PRAYER ACCEPTABLY?

1. A sense of our necessities; for until we feel our wants we never shall pray with any fervency. So long as we are sipping at every accessible fountain of earthly pleasure and getting up for ourselves poor broken cisterns besides, we are never likely to come to the gospel fountain. The soul needs to have a sense of its great necessities. It needs a consciousness of being altogether empty, and therefore a conviction of its need of access to the divine fountain, or there is not hope it will ever come to this fountain for the waters of life.

2. Another requisite is a sense of dependence on God for this state of mind. Persons may feel their need of the blessing, and yet may not realize their dependence on God. Nevertheless, this feeling of dependence must exist in the mind before one can deeply and earnestly rest upon God for the blessing.

Men need to know and to realize that although they have power to repent, they cannot get access to this fountain of divine pleasures without God's help. His angel must come down and trouble the waters of this "house of mercy," and lend us a kind hand to help us down therein.' Then our soul is made whole of "whatsoever disease it had."

3. **Acceptable prayer implies fulfilling the conditions.** Otherwise, we only tempt God. Someone who knows the revealed conditions, and yet prays for God to bestow the blessing without fulfilling the conditions, insults God to His face. It amounts to demanding that God retreat from His expressed conditions; a thing which of course He never can do, and which no man can even impliedly ask Him to do without abusing his God exceedingly.

Especially is it important that this prayer be not selfish. The soul must be consecrated to God and fully purposed to use the blessing, if obtained or not obtained, yet to use everything it has, for the glory of God and the highest good of man. So David felt. "Then will I teach transgressors thy ways, and sinners shall be converted unto thee."

There is the greatest danger in asking for spiritual joy, that our hearts will be merely selfish in it. Instead, we should fair-mindedly seek to glorify God in all things, even with the religious joy and peace that He may graciously impart to us.

4. **A sense of its great value is another requisite.** This should be coupled with a deep sense of ill-desert. Combining these two

sentiments in their great strength, you then have a state of mind in which you are in small danger of seeking in vain.

5. In connection with these, there must be great confidence in God's willingness to bestow the blessings sought. David seems to have had this.

6. Also, a willingness to have God employ all the necessary means to open the way for this result. There may be a great many springs of earthly joy to be dried up, many idols to be removed, and many a cup of earthly pleasure to be dashed before we are prepared to receive in our souls the joy of God's salvation. Consequently, there must be a willingness to have God do anything He pleases to prepare our souls.

Unless we are thus willing that God should take His own course, we are making conditions for God that show that we are real hypocrites. We are trying to get the joy of holiness without the holiness itself.

7. There must also be a willingness to leave the time, the way, and the conditions of conferring the blessing wholly in the disposal of Infinite Wisdom. All must be left in His hands with most unqualified submission, ready to do or suffer anything that is necessary, that we may most glorify God.

8. There must be a fixed purpose to make wise and holy use of the blessings that we receive. It must be in our heart to use this blessing wholly for God. Unless we pray for it with the sincere intention of asking it thus for God, we have no reason whatever to expect it.

A man would be but poorly employed in praying for this blessing to put it under a bushel. The great Giver would fain make

His goodness known; and why should not you lend your aid in so noble an enterprise, for an end so glorious?

If God fills your cup, you must be willing to pass it around and let all others be refreshed from the same fountain. Show them where the fountain is, and how good its waters are. They do not know much about these things, and they need such hints as you can easily give them, if your own heart is full of that divine joy.

REMARKS

1. Many professors of religion know nothing of the joys of God's salvation. I recollect to have been impressed with this long before my conversion. At that time I was in the habit of conversing with Christians about their own experience. Having much curiosity on this subject I felt free to inquire about it and took frequent opportunities to do so. It was with me then, a matter of speculation, as I was then, as now, much struck with the apparent fact that so few Christians had much real joy in God. The impression was often made on my mind that most Christians were wretched, unhappy, muttering, grumbling, and full of trouble.

Therefore, the conviction ripened more and more on my mind that they had little or no real joy in God. They might have repented of sin, and lost their burden at the cross; but yet they seemed not to know much if anything about the joys of God's salvation. On this subject they were generally dumb, having little or nothing to say of the salvation of God, and the light of His countenance.

2. A great many professors of religion seem not to care for this blessing. They scramble after dress or money, as anxious after worldly good as if there were no other good for them to seek and as anxious for this world as if God had told them to seek first the kingdom of this world and its good things. Therefore, they press on, running to this concert, to that show or party of pleasure, always lusting after something sensual and worldly. Such are their pursuits, and such of course is their character.

This kind of person would much rather go to a circus than into their closet, or to a prayer meeting. They cannot imagine how any man can wish to go like Francis Xavier into his closet, and spend seven hours at once in such deep and holy communion with God that his countenance glowed like an angel's. They can form no just conception of the attractiveness of such a scene and of such employments.

3. When a Christian has really tasted this joy in God, and then subsequently has been deprived of it, he will go with his head bowed down like a bulrush. He looks as if he has lost all the friends he ever had. Having once drunk of the sweet waters of life, O how insipid is the draught of earthly joy!

I do not mean to imply by this that Christians cannot enjoy earthly things. They can. None can enjoy earthly good with half so solid a relish as they when they can have God in all their earthly good, and take all as His gift, and from His hand. But let a man who has experienced these joys, once get away from God, away into sin as David did, and his peace and joy are spoiled. He looks ashamed before God and before men and cannot hold up his head. If you meet him in a Christian spirit, he cannot look you in the face, especially if you show him that your heart is full of the joys of God's salvation.

How often have I seen this; and so probably have many of you. Look around you. There is a professed Christian, fallen into sin. Let one arise before him, full of the joys of God's salvation, and Oh, how self-condemned he is. How full of agony and trouble! Poor man; he is far from God and can find no rest there.

4. Some persons care just enough for these joys to pray for them selfishly, but in no other way. Most of you who are present today will recollect that I stated a fact here some weeks ago that may apply well here. A man with whom I was boarding in a season of revival, being greatly troubled about his own spiritual state, said to me, "What would you think of a man who prays for the Spirit of God week after week, but never gets it?"

My reply was, "I should think the man prayed selfishly. I presume that is all the trouble. The devil might pray for spiritual joy in the very same way. His only planned objective being his own spiritual enjoyment. The Psalmist did not pray so. He did indeed pray that God would restore to him the lost joys of his salvation; but his motives in it were not selfish, for he adds, Then will I teach transgressors thy ways, and sinners shall be converted unto thee."

This seemed to the man a hard saying, and he went away, as he afterwards told me, in great anger, and prayed that God would kill him. A little more thought however, together with the melting power of the Spirit, subdued him, and he became as docile and humble as a lamb.

So it often happens that men want God to meet their selfishness; and when they find He does not, they have often a long struggle before they really humble themselves, so as to meet God on His own ground.

5. Many think that all caring for the joy of God's salvation is necessarily selfish. They do not realize the value of this joy to the church, to God, and to the world, and hence they cannot realize that any other than selfish motives can induce Christians to pray for it. Consequently, with these views of the selfish character, they pray for it very little, if at all.

Again, few realize the importance of having this joy of the Lord in their souls. They seem not to appreciate its important bearings upon the interests of vital godliness.

Many Christians have special seasons and states of mind in which they are very desirous to have this blessing; but on the whole they are unwilling to yield up the sources of their carnal joys. They would gladly have both if they could. However, since they cannot be, they cleave to the carnal, and forgo the spiritual. A most unwise, most wretched, and most guilty choice!

Again, spiritual joy often abounds when all other sources of joy are dried up. By this, I do not mean that joy in God precludes all enjoyment of the world and its pleasures; for this is very far from being true. My meaning is that when worldly sources of pleasure are cut off from us or are dried up, then God comes in to fill the void with richer spiritual joys.

Poverty and losses may have withdrawn from you many of the comforts of life. Nevertheless, God can make His grace to abound so much the more, that your soul shall rejoice exceedingly in the exchange. Sickness may have robbed you of the joy that health affords, but God can make your soul prosper and be in health to such a degree that your physical loss shall be more than counter-balanced by your spiritual gain.

God knows how to fill up the chasms of earthly happiness that His providence makes. Often He makes them for the very purpose apparently of filling them with the more precious material of His own spiritual blessings. He sometimes finds Himself under the necessity of cutting off every source of earthly joy in order that He may shut us up utterly to Himself.

When He finds us unwilling to let go of earthly idols, God leaves them to their own choice, saying, "They have loved idols and after them they will go." "They are joined to their idols. Let them alone." However, if we are willing to serve God, then we may find sources of spiritual joy springing up in the most barren of earth's deserts. Nothing earthly is so desolate that God cannot gladden it with the intermingled joys of His salvation.

On the other hand, if you will selfishly cleave to earth, and thrust away the offered joys of God's love, then if He would save you, there remains no alternative but to scatter desolation broadcast over all your earthly joys. God will blight them if He can. And surely, He who has the resources of the universe at His command can never lack the means of filling your cup with dregs of wormwood and gall. It would be the worst form of folly if you should compel your loving Father to do this as a last resort in order to save and bless your soul.

Again, very few realize how much the absence of spiritual joy and its manifestations dishonour God. Few realize how great a stumbling block it is to men to see professed Christians go about with a heart all sorrowful, bowed down and hatefully selfish. Many show no trust, or almost none, in God; no joy in the light of His countenance; and no preparation of heart for doing anything efficiently in God's service. It is a living reproach to the name of Jesus, that His people should appear thus before either their brethren or the world.

Legalists are greatly stumbled at those who possess the joy of God's salvation. Legalists are never happy in themselves but always in a straitjacket with every muscle drawn up with a tightness never to be relaxed. They do not know about such a joyous state of mind. They see a great many things that look suspicious.

When they see souls rejoicing greatly in the Lord, oh, they don't know about that. If a Christian's soul triumphs in his God, alas, they say to themselves, what can that mean? There is nothing like that in my religion! There is quite too much cheerfulness often in other people's religion to suit their taste, or to tally with their own experience. Never having had any experience in such joys as those, they are greatly scandalized.

It seems to have been this way with one of David's wives, when she saw him running and dancing before the ark of the Lord in the overflowings of his joy. Indeed, she thought, this looks very unbecoming for a king, for the king of Israel.

Christians of a somber, heavy countenance, who have never known anything of the gladsome joy of holy love, cannot even explain to themselves the peaceful look of the saint who is communing with God. Above all, these who do not know the first element of someone's state of mind whose soul pours forth the gushing tides of its affection before God, those who look on amazed at such manifestations because they know nothing of them in their own experience will doubtless be greatly stumbled.

But notwithstanding all their stumbling, if this spiritual joy is sustained by a holy consistent life, it cannot fail to exert its power upon their hearts. They maybe at first offended, but soon they must see that there is both reason and reality in the peaceful joy of those who walk humbly with God. O Lord, they will be compelled to say, I do not know that experience. I am a stranger to something. I must know what that is. I doubt whether my religion is worth a straw. Sure, I am that it gives me no joy in the Lord like what I see in those other Christians.

Few things are a greater curse than a legal state of mind. It is often as bad as open wickedness, if not worse. Often it is such a misrepresentation of religion as makes the little children more afraid of such a religious man than of a fiend. Does he recommend religion? He could not possibly disparage and misrepresent it more than he does.

Far better if he were never thought to be a Christian at all;

for then his somber, morose and harsh spirit would be ascribed to its true cause, the selfishness of his heart and the utter absence of the gentle spirit of gospel love. Many fail of this joy because they do not ask for it. Will you, my hearers, lose it through lack of prayer and of faith? It is too choice a blessing to be missed for such a reason.

4

THE REWARD OF FERVENT PRAYER

Delivered May 15, 1850 at the Tabernacle, Moorfields.
The Penny Pulpit, No.1522

"Open thy mouth wide, and I will fill it"
—Psalm 81:10

These words were addressed by God to the Church. There is nothing in the context in which they are found that particularly demands explanation. I would, therefore, proceed at once to say that this promise and injunction being addressed to the Church was also, of course, addressed to individual Christians. Whenever a promise or an injunction is applicable to the Church, it is also applicable to each individual composing the Church. This reveals to us the principle on which God deals with His people. The spirit of what is written here is even more true. In briefly considering this subject, I propose to show:

1. What this language means.

2. What it implies.

3. What its relationship is to our responsibilities.

1. WHAT THIS LANGUAGE MEANS

Of course, it is figurative. "Open thy mouth wide, and I will fill it." Does this mean literally open the mouth wide and He will fill it with some unknown thing?

"I am the Lord thy God, which brought thee out of the land of Egypt."

This was addressed to the Church of old, and the spirit of it is addressed to the Church in all ages. It is said in the eighth verse, "Hear, O my people, and I will testify unto thee: O Israel, if thou wilt hearken unto me; there shall no strange god be in thee; neither shalt thou worship any strange god. I am the Lord thy God, which brought thee out of the land of Egypt: open thy mouth wide and I will fill it." The language, then, is figurative, and is to be understood in the following ways.

God instructs us to ask of Him great things. The injunction is not only, "Open thy mouth," but also open it wide; open it fully to its utmost capacity. By this, it is to be understood that we are to ask of God great things; as great as we can conceive. We are merely creatures, therefore our conceptions are low, and the spirit of the injunction tells us that we should ask great things of our heavenly Father.

With our finite powers, we can conceive of Him "who is able to do for us abundantly above all that we can ask or think." Let the request be ever so great, He can grant it. In your petitions to Him, therefore, "open thy mouth wide," ask for things as great as you can conceive.

Another thing we are to understand by this language is that we are to expect those great things for which we ask. We are required to ask believingly in expectation that He will give the things that we ask.

The spirit of this injunction also means that we are to attempt to accomplish great things for God. We are to ask earnestly, largely, and perseveringly in order that we may honour and glorify Him. Here, I might add, we are to understand that all our petitions must be addressed in the name of Christ from right motives.

2. WHAT "OPEN THY MOUTH WIDE" IMPLIES

The injunction "open thy mouth wide" is followed by the promise "and I will fill it."

This language implies that God is interested in us. What would motivate Him to say this to us if He were not interested in us? Why should He exhort us to open our mouths wide and ask of Him great things if He had no interest in us? This language must surely imply that for some reason or other He has great interest in His Church, and, of course, in each individual composing that Church.

It implies that He is interested in those things He requires us to do. He is interested in giving us the great things that He has promised, and in our possessing them to enable us to do what He requires of us.

GOD'S FULL PROVISION

God has made provision for us in every situation. He does not require great things of His people without promising the grace to help them perform that which He requires of them. However, He does require many and great things of His people. He requires them to go forth to conquer the world, and many other things He requires of them in the various relations that they sustain to the world and to society.

Now, you must not complain that you cannot accomplish what is required of you, that you cannot do this or that because of your littleness or insufficiency. For God says, open your mouth wide for ability to do His will and He will fill it. He will enable you to do what is required of you. Therefore, this language implies His interest in us personally, and that He is greatly interested in giving us the things for which we ask. He is quite able to supply all our need out of His fullness and to give us everything we want to enable us to accomplish everything He requires of us.

This language is addressed to different classes of individuals who maintain particular relations in life regarding special and particular circumstances. For example, it is addressed to local authorities, ministers, parents, and private Christians. Whatever the circumstances, this language relates to your particular needs: "open thy mouth wide, and I will fill it."

It is of great importance for everyone to understand that God is interested in each individual. He takes all things into account. He placed us in our various relations; therefore, He must be interested in us. He is able to make His grace sufficient to enable us to do all that is required of us so we may honour and glorify His name. People can never be too well assured of this: "I am Jehovah, thy God." What is implied in that? "Thy God." "Open thy mouth wide," therefore, "and I will fill it." These words apply to every individual in all the relations of life.

Now, think of what your relations are. Think of your personal circumstances, peculiar trials, difficulties, responsibilities, and the duties you are called upon to perform, no matter what they are. Only understand God as addressing you by name, whether old, young, rich, poor, influential or otherwise, no matter. Only understand God as saying to you, "I am Jehovah, thy God: open thy mouth wide, and I will fill it." He is interested in your maintaining these responsibilities in a manner worthy of Him, as being His children.

I have often thought of the magnitude of unbelief. The unbelief of many is so great that they entirely overlook the secret depths of meaning that the promises of God contain, and they stumble at some of the plainest things in the Bible.

Suppose the King of England should send his son to travel on the Continent or in America, and should say to him, "Now, son, you are going among strangers, so remember your great responsibilities: you are my son, and you are my representative. When the people see you they will form an opinion of me, and they will estimate my character very much by yours, as a natural consequence. Now, remember, wherever you are, that the eyes of the people are upon you and my honour is concerned in your behavior. I have great interest in you; first, because you are my son; and second, because you are to be my representative among those who do not know me personally. I am, therefore, greatly concerned that you should not misrepresent me. For particular and weighty reasons, therefore, I want you to conduct yourself like a prince, and that you may do so, you shall always have the means. Remember never to exercise any kind of economy that will disgrace your father and the nation you represent. Draw upon me liberally. Of course, you will not squander needlessly upon your lusts, for such conduct would disgrace yourself and dishonour me: but what you want for the purpose of representing fully the Sovereign of England you can have. Draw largely; always remember this."

Now observe. God has placed His people here in a world of strangers to Him. He has placed them in various relations. He has admonished them to remember that they are His children and they are also His representatives in this world. God says to them, "I have placed you in these relations that you may honour me. I love you as my own children. I have given my Son to redeem you, and thus I have proved my personal regard for you. I always desire that you should walk worthy of the high vocation wherewith you are called. Remember, you are my representatives in the midst of a rebellious world; therefore, 'let your light so shine before men, that others, seeing your good works, may glorify your Father which is in heaven.'"

God's own interest in us leads Him to tell us to ask largely of Him. His intrinsic regard for us as our Father, as His redeemed children, is very great. Indeed, from every perspective, He has the deepest interest in us. So that we will not dishonour Him, He tells us He will give us grace to meet all our responsibilities and discharge our duties. "Open your mouths wide," He says, "and I will fill them." "I will supply all your needs. I am glad to do it. I shall delight to do it. I am interested in doing it."

Now, do not ever forget this. Ask largely enough, ask confidently enough, and ask perseveringly enough to meet all your needs. I suppose that no one is likely to call in question the truth of any of these principles.

These words, "open thy mouth wide, and I will fill it," imply that provision is made to supply our needs. In addition, it implies that God's capability is so great that He does not fear that we shall need anything, or be able to conceive of anything, beyond His power to grant. Hence, He tells us that His grace is sufficient for us.

Observe, He does not caution us about asking too much, but He tells us here, as in many other parts of the Bible, to make our requests unlimited. "Ask what you will, and it shall be done unto you." Of course it means, "what you will" for a right reason, not for a selfish and improper reason.

We are not restricted at all in Him. It is not intended that we should hesitate to accomplish anything that He requires of us. We are not restricted in Him, for He says, "Open thy mouth wide, and I will fill it." In any of the circumstances or relations in which we may ever be placed, or whatever we may be called upon to accomplish, we are never to regard ourselves as restricted in Him.

If He requires His people to go forth to the conquest of the world, they are abundantly able to take possession of the land. We are to have confidence in Him, and to take possession of it in His name and in His strength. If He tells us to compass the city and blow with the ram's horns, the walls of Jericho shall surely tumble down-there is no mistake about it.

In this injunction and promise is implied that if we fail in any way to perfectly represent or obey Him in every respect, or fail to be and do what He requires of us, the fault is not His but ours. It is not to be resolved into "the mysterious sovereignty of God," for the fault is ours. If we fail, it is not because God, by any arbitrary sovereignty, withheld the power, but because as a matter of fact, in the possession of our liberty we failed to believe and appropriate the promises.

GOD IS HONOURED BY BIG REQUESTS

This injunction and promise implies that God considers Himself honoured by the largeness of our requests. If we ask but a trifling thing, it shows that we find ourselves either unable or unwilling to expect or believe any great thing of Him.

What does it imply when people ask small favors of God? I know very well what people say. They say they are so unworthy that they cannot expect to get any great things in answer to their poor requests. However, is this real humility, or is it a voluntary humility? Is it a commendable state of mind? "Our prayers are so poor, are so unworthy, that we cannot expect to receive much in answer to them. Therefore, we have not confidence enough to ask great things, and so we only ask for small things that we may without presumption expect to receive."

Is this a right disposition of mind? This is, in fact, that voluntary humility that God denounces. It is self-righteousness. What state of mind must that individual be in, who, instead of measuring his requests by the greatness of God's mercies, the greatness of His promises and the largeness of His heart, shall measure them by his own worthiness or unworthiness? Why, the fact is, if an individual will measure his requests by such a standard, he will ask nothing better than hell, and he may expect nothing better. This is applicable to all men in all ages, if they make themselves the standard of their requests.

However, if we are to rely upon God's promises, faithfulness, abounding grace in Christ Jesus and eternal love, then there are infinite blessings in store for His people. Moreover, the goodness of His heart is trying to force these blessings upon them. Then what has our great unworthiness to do but to commend us to God's grace and mercy?

Therefore, whenever we ask great things of God, and expect great things from Him, we honour Him. We are, in fact, saying, "Lord, although we are infinitely unholy and unworthy of thy blessings, yet we judge not of what thou art willing to give us, measured by our unworthiness, but by thine own wonderful love to the world as shown in the gift of thine own and well-beloved Son, the Lord Jesus Christ. Therefore, we will not ask small things of so great a God. We will ask great things because it is in thine heart to give them, and thou findest it more blessed to give than we do to receive." Now, it is by this sort of confidence that we honour God.

Some ask scantily, sparingly, for fear of overtaxing or overburdening God. What a mean, low, and contemptible view this is of God! Suppose the prince, whom we referred to, had been very sparing in drawing upon his father's accounts. Suppose that he drew only five or ten dollars at a time. The strangers among whom he was living would have noticed it. They would have said, "What can it mean? Why does he not draw more? How is he so poor? Is his father so miserly or so poor?" Thus, dishonour would be brought upon his father and his country because the prince drew so sparingly when he might have had plenty.

Now, God has sent His children to this land, and He has told them that they are the "light of the world," the "salt of the earth," a "city that is set upon a hill." In addition, He says, "Let your light shine"; show yourselves worthy of your heavenly Father. Now, suppose that from a lack of confidence, or for some other reason, they draw very sparingly. Everybody will see that they get but little from God in answer to prayer.

A miserable, lean, famishing supply is all these people get from their heavenly Father. They have so little grace, faith and anything that one might suppose God would surely provide for His children; there is only a slight spiritual distinction between them and the world they live in. Is this honourable to God?

How can you profess to be children of God and never realize your high distinction? Living in a world of rebels and having no more grace than you have, you never thought of the dishonour you bring upon God. What do you think of your Father? Do you think that God your Father is satisfied? To see you, people would think you had no Father, that you were poor orphans.

And yet God says, "Open thy mouth wide, and I will fill it; ask of me such things as you need. Why, then, do you go about in such a miserable condition? Why live at such a dying rate, always in doubt, darkness and trouble? Do you not know that I am the Lord your God, and that if you open your mouth wide, I will fill it?"

Now, brethren, is this not true? Is this some newfangled doctrine not taught in the Bible? Or have professing Christians generally infinitely misconceived this matter, not understanding what God requires of them, or that they have dishonoured Him to the highest degree by such conduct. They the light of the world! Why, their lamps are gone out! They cannot get any oil; and if they could, they have no money to buy it.

Why is your lamp gone out? Has God your Father failed to send you a remittance? In any event, the lamp has gone out and left you in obscure darkness so a worldly spirit has come over you. What is the matter? You have been going by little and little until you have lost almost all confidence in God, and scarcely expect to receive anything from Him in answer to your prayers.

I do not know how it is with you, but I know that the great mass of professing Christians is in this miserably low state. They seem neither to know that they dishonour God by their conduct, nor that God is ready and willing to give them abundance of grace if they will believingly seek for it.

Of course, if God considers Himself honoured by the largeness of our requests, it must be upon the condition that we really have confidence in Him. We are expecting to receive those things for which we ask. If we should ask great things in words but not mean what we ask, or if we do not expect to receive answers to our petitions, we dishonour God by mocking Him. Always observe and remember this: a man who really expects great things from God and asks of God in faith with right motives will receive them. Those who honour God, God will honour.

God regards Himself as honoured by everything we accomplish in His name: by our asking great things of Him, and by our attempting great things in His name.

GOD IS DISHONOURED BY FEEBLE REQUESTS

Suppose a man goes forth in the name of the Lord Jesus to carry the Gospel to those who are in darkness, believing what Jesus has said, "Lo, I am with you always, even unto the end of the world." Suppose that in this confidence he attempts great things, and aims at the conquest of cities and nations. The greater his aim in God's name and strength, so much the greater is the honour that God receives.

He goes forth relying on God, as God's servant, as God's child, to accomplish great things in His name and strength. God considers Himself honoured by this. God considers Himself honoured by the high attainments of His children and dishonoured by their low attainments. He is honoured in the fact that their graces so shine forth that it shall be seen by all around that they have partaken largely of His Spirit.

Exalted piety is honourable to God. Manifestations of great grace and spirituality of mind honour God. He is greatly honoured by the fruits of righteousness His people bring forth. Christ Himself says, "Herein is my Father glorified that ye bring forth much fruit."

Ministers should be greatly fruitful. They should bring forth the fruits of the Spirit in their tempers, in their lives, in the strength of their faith and labors of love. Can you doubt that God has great interest in these things? Indeed His great desire, that you should bring forth fruit to His glory, is shown in the fact that He says, "open thy mouth wide, and I will fill it."

It must also imply that He is greatly dishonoured by the opposite of this. Professing Christians who have but little faith make but feeble efforts, and have but very little to distinguish them from the world around them. Nothing can be more offensive to God than for His professed servants to have so little confidence in Him that they ask sparingly to receive sparingly. It must be admitted, I suppose, that the conceptions of the general population of Christians are very low. They expect but small things from God.

However, this is dishonourable to God, and He is endeavoring by every possible means to encourage our faith. In one instance, He will go into the nursery, where the mother is with her children, and say, "Mother, if thy son should ask for bread, would you give him a stone? Or if he should ask a fish, would you give him a serpent? Or if he should ask an egg, would you give him a scorpion to sting him to death?"

The mother is surprised, and can scarcely contain herself. "Well," He says, "I know you would not do these things, but if these things would be far from you and you feel indignant at the bare suggestion of the possibility, 'how much more will your heavenly Father give good things to them that ask him?'" "How much?" Why, as much as He is better than you are.

A parent has no higher happiness than to give his little ones what they ask for if it is for their good. A father or a mother purchases some dainty thing and they can hardly bear to taste it themselves because the children must have it. "If ye, then, being evil" (compared with God, infinitely evil) "know how to give good gifts unto your children, how much more shall your heavenly Father give..." What? Oranges, sweets, candy. No, "...the Holy Spirit to them that ask Him." That is the great blessing that you need. Oh, if we could only have more of the Spirit!

Christians live as if God had only a little of the Holy Spirit to give. Is this the representation of the Scriptures? No, the scriptures indicate infinitely the reverse of this. Some professing Christians live like spiritual skeletons, and, if they are reproved for it, they say, "Oh, we are dependent on the Holy Spirit."

Indeed, and is that the reason you are so much like the world? You do not prevail with God to convert your children, and the clerks and people around you? Grieve not the Holy Spirit with such excuses. Seek, and ye shall find. God is infinitely more ready to give you His Holy Spirit than you are to give good gifts to your own children.

When God exhorts His people to open their mouths wide, and promises to fill them, we are to understand that He seeks in them a clear medium through which to communicate His blessings to those around them. This is a natural law of the divine economy. If you are parents and have unconverted children, or have those around you unconverted, God seeks to make you an agent by which He can communicate the blessings of salvation to them.

When God thus urges people to open their mouths wide in order that He may fill them, we are to understand that His heart is very much set upon their having the things which He is seeking to give them. He takes the highest interest in their having these things, in fact, a greater interest than they do themselves. He restrains not His gift at all; the infinite fountain of His love and blessing flows everlastingly, so that every empty vessel may be filled; and, when they are all full, this living stream still flows on forever.

We must not be afraid of asking too much. When we seek a favor from a finite being, we might ask so much as to seem unreasonable; but when we come to an infinite being, we cannot ask too largely. Oh, brethren, always remember that.

3. OUR RESPONSIBILITIES

We are entirely without excuse to God for not being and doing what would satisfy His divine mind in the highest degree. We are not restricted in Him, but in ourselves.

We are not only without excuse to God, but we are cruel to ourselves. How cruel a man would be to himself if he starved himself to death in the midst of plenty, of which he might freely partake? Now, what excuse can a Christian have for all his doubts, fears, darkness and perplexities? How cruel he is to himself when such marvelous provision is made to set the Christian free from all such unhappy experiences. Do we live under such circumstances, and yet have a life of complaining? Indeed! In addition, is it a law of God's house that His children almost starve? Is it a rule of God's house that His children should not have grace enough to lift them above perplexities and unbelief?

Does God starve His children to death? The voice of the devil says, "They do all they can; can't they get grace enough to prevent their living so much like my own servants? So much alike are they, indeed, that nobody can distinguish them from my children!" Dear children, is there not an infinite mistake here? Are we not dishonouring God if we do not avail ourselves of the great things that God has provided us?

It is cruelty to the world also. God has said, "Go forth, and conquer the world and disciple all nations." Has He said this to His people, and do they slumber, do they hesitate? What is the matter, brethren? Are not the words, "Come over and help us," borne on the four winds of heaven? "Come over into Macedonia and help us." Send us missionaries, Bibles, tracts, and send us the Gospel. Is the Church unable to do it? What is the matter? Do let me ask, is there not something entirely wrong here? Does God require His people to make brick without straw? Has the world any right to expect the gospel of salvation to be sent to them by the Church? Brethren, consider!

What cruelty it is to those around us and those who sustain relations to us. We have such a promise in the Bible, yet our children remain unconverted! Think of it!

If Christians would but avail themselves of all the blessings which God has provided and really become filled with the Spirit, what do you suppose would be the result? Let me ask this question, "Suppose every Christian in your city should really comply with the appeal and be filled with the Holy Spirit? What do you suppose would be the natural effect upon the populace?

Suppose every Christian were to open His mouth wide, and should receive the Holy Spirit. Do you not believe that in one year a very great change would occur in the city, so that you would scarcely recognize it? I have not the least doubt that more good would be done than has been done before in your city. If one church could be thoroughly awakened, another and another would follow, until the whole city would be aroused and every chapel would be filled with devout inquirers after salvation. This has been the case frequently in American cities; and the same may occur in any city if Christians are only thoroughly alive to their duties and responsibilities.

If every Christian in your city would make up his mind to take hold of the promise of God, and thus come into deep sympathy and fellowship with Him, the effect would be astonishing. Like the lamps of the city, Christians are scattered over it so they may give light to the multitudes around them. However, if they are not lighted up, the purpose for which they were intended is not accomplished. Let every Christian in your city be filled with the Holy Spirit, and what would be the result? Your city would move! Your state would move! America would move! Europe would move! Asia would move! The world would move!

Now, brethren, does this appear extravagant? If so, it is because you do not consider the power of God's promises and what churches are able to accomplish in His name. The guilt and the weakness of the Church is her unbelief. This is so great that she does not expect to do much.

REMARKS

Many people so confound faith with sight that they are ready to say, "If God should make windows in heaven, then might this thing be true." A great many people have no faith except in connection with sight. If you give them the naked promise, they cannot believe it; they must have something they can see. Few individuals can walk by faith, but when they see a thing accomplished, they think they have strong faith. Nevertheless, only let this appearance be put out of sight and their faith is gone again.

Now, what a Christian ought to be able to do is this: take God's promises and anchor right down upon them without waiting to see anything. Somebody must believe simply on the strength of God's testimony, somebody must begin by naked faith, or there will be no visible testimony.

God always honours real faith. He is concerned to do so. God often greatly honours the faith of His people. He frequently gives them more than they expect. People will pray for one individual, and God will often honour their faith by not only converting that individual but many others also.

I once knew a man who was sick, and a neighbor of his, an unconverted man, frequently sent from his store things for his comfort. This poor man said to himself, "I cannot repay Mr. Chandler for his kindness, but I will give myself up to pray for him." To the surprise of all the neighborhood, Mr. Chandler became converted. When he testified of this before the whole congregation, it had such an effect that a great revival ensued and many souls were brought to God. This poor man gave himself up to pray for one individual, and God honoured his faith by converting many, thus fulfilling the declaration of His Word, that He will "do exceeding abundantly above all we can ask or think."

Instead of finding that God gives grudgingly and sparingly, He gives abundantly. God always acts worthy of Himself. You ask a blessing of God in faith and He says, "Be content, and take a great deal more so that your cup shall run over." The fact is, where but little is attempted, little expected, little will be received; but where little is really obtained, the fault is not with God, but entirely with us.

5

THE PRAYER OF FAITH

"Therefore I say unto you, What things so ever ye desire when ye pray, believe that ye receive them, and ye shall have them."

—Mark 11:24

These words have been supposed by some to refer exclusively to the faith of miracles. However, there is not the least evidence of this. That the text was not designed by our Saviour to refer exclusively to the faith of miracles is proved by the connection in which it stands.

If you read the chapter, you will see that Christ and His apostles, as they returned from their place of retirement in the morning, faint and hungry, saw a fig tree at a little distance. It looked very beautiful, and doubtless gave signs of having fruit on it. But when they came nigh, they found nothing on it but leaves. And Jesus said: "No man eat fruit of thee hereafter for ever. And His disciples heard it" (Mark 11:14).

"And in the morning, as they passed by, they saw the fig-tree dried up from the roots.

"And Peter calling to remembrance saith unto Him, Master, behold, the fig-tree which Thou cursed is withered away.

"And Jesus answering saith unto them, Have faith in God.

"For verily I say unto you, That whosoever shall say unto this mountain, Be thou removed, and be thou cast into the sea; and shall not doubt in his heart, but shall believe that those things which he saith shall come to pass; he shall have whatsoever he saith" (Mark 11:20-23).

Then follow the words of the text: "Therefore I say unto you, What things so ever ye desire when ye pray, believe that ye receive them, and ye shall have them."

Our Saviour was desirous of giving His disciples instructions respecting the nature and power of prayer, and the necessity of strong faith in God. He therefore stated a very strong case; a miracle as great as the removal of a mountain into the sea. In addition, He tells them, that if they exercise a proper faith in God, they might do such things.

But His remarks are not to be limited to faith merely in regard to working miracles, for He goes on to say: "And when ye stand praying, forgive, if ye have ought against any: that your Father also which is in heaven may forgive you your trespasses. But if ye do not forgive, neither will your Father which is in heaven forgive your trespasses" (25-26).

Does that relate to miracles? When you pray, you must forgive. Is that required only when a man wishes to work a miracle? There are many other promises in the Bible closely related to this, and speaking nearly the same language, which have been all dismissed in this way, as referring to the faith employed in miracles. Just as if the faith of miracles was something different from faith in God!

I propose to show:

1. That faith is an indispensable condition of prevailing prayer.

2. What it is that we are to believe when we pray.

3. When we are bound to exercise this faith, or to believe that we shall receive the thing we ask for.

4. That this kind of faith in prayer always does obtain the blessing sought.

I also propose:

5. To explain how we are to come into the state of mind in which we can exercise such faith; and,

6. To answer several objections, which are sometimes alleged against these views of prayer.

1. FAITH AN INDISPENSABLE CONDITION.

That this is so will not be seriously doubted, there is such a thing as offering benevolent desires, which are acceptable to God as such, that do not include the exercise of faith in regard to the actual reception of those blessings. However, such desires are not prevailing prayer, the prayer of faith.

God may see fit to grant the things desired, as an act of kindness and love, but it would not be properly in answer to prayer. I am speaking now of the kind of faith that ensures the blessing. Do not understand me as saying that there is nothing in prayer that is acceptable to God, or that even obtains the blessing sometimes, without this kind of faith. I am speaking of the faith that secures the very blessing it seeks.

To prove that faith is indispensable to prevailing prayer, it is only necessary to repeat what the apostle James expressly tells us: "If any of you lack wisdom, let him ask of God, that giveth to all men liberally, and upbraideth not; and it shall be given him. But let him ask in faith, nothing wavering. For he that wavereth, is like a wave of the sea driven with the wind and tossed" (James 1:5-6)

2. WHAT WE ARE TO BELIEVE WHEN WE PRAY.

We are to believe in the existence of God. "He that cometh to God must believe that He is," and in His willingness to answer prayer, "that He is, and that He is a rewarder of them that diligently seek Him" (Hebrews 11:6). There are many who believe in the existence of God, but do not believe in the efficacy of prayer. They profess to believe in God, but deny the necessity or influence of prayer.

We are to believe that we shall receive something ... what? Not something, or anything, as it happens; but some particular thing we ask for. We are not to think that God is such a Being, that if we ask a fish, He will give us a serpent; or if we ask bread, He will give us a stone. But He says: "What things so ever ye desire when ye pray, believe that ye receive them, and ye shall have them." With respect to the faith of miracles, it is plain that the disciples were bound to believe they should receive just what they asked for. In other words, the very thing itself should come to pass.

That is what they were to believe. Now, what ought men to believe in regard to other blessings? Is it a mere loose idea, that if a man prays for a specific blessing, God will by some mysterious sovereignty give something or other to him, or something to somebody else, somewhere?

When a man prays for his children's conversion, is he to believe that either his children will be converted or somebody else's children, altogether uncertain which? No, this is utter nonsense, and highly dishonourable to God. We are to believe that we shall receive the very things that we ask for.

3. WHEN ARE WE BOUND TO MAKE THIS PRAYER?

When are we bound to believe that we shall have the very things we pray for? I answer: "When we have evidence of it." Faith must always have evidence. A man cannot believe a thing, unless he sees something that he supposes to be evidence. He is under no obligation to believe, and has no right to believe a thing will be done, unless he has evidence. It is the height of fanaticism to believe without evidence. The kinds of evidence a man may have are the following:

Suppose that God has especially promised the thing. Take, for instance, when God says He is more ready to give His Holy Spirit to them that ask Him, than parents are to give bread to their children. Here we are bound to believe that we shall receive it when we pray for it. You have no right to insert an "if" and say, "Lord, if it be Thy will, give us Thy Holy Spirit."

This is to insult God. To put "if" into God's promise, where God has put none, is tantamount to charging God with being insincere. It is like saying: "O God, if Thou art in earnest in making these promises, grant us the blessing we pray for."

I heard of a case where a young convert was used to teach a minister a solemn truth on the subject of prayer. She was from a very wicked family, but went to live at a minister's house. While there she was hopefully converted. One day she went to the minister's study while he was there, a thing she was not in the habit of doing. He thought there must be something the matter with her, so he asked her to sit down, and kindly inquired into the state of her religious feelings.

She told him that she was distressed at the manner in which the older Church members prayed for the Spirit. They would pray for the Holy Spirit to come, and would seem to be very much in earnest, and plead the promises of God. Then they would say: "O Lord, if it be Thy will, grant us these blessings for Christ's sake." She thought that saying, "If it be Thy will," when God had expressly promised it was questioning whether God was sincere in His promises.

The minister tried to reason her out of it, and he succeeded in confounding her. However, she was distressed and filled with grief, and said: "I cannot argue the point with you, sir, but it is impressed on my mind that it is wrong and dishonouring to God." Eventually, she went away, weeping with anguish. The minister saw she was not satisfied, and it led him to look at the matter again.

Finally, the minister saw that it was putting in an "if" where God had put none, except where He had revealed His will expressly; and he saw that it was an insult to God. Thereupon he went and told his people they were bound to believe that God was in earnest when He made them a promise. As a result, the spirit of prayer came down upon that Church, and a most powerful revival followed.

Where there is a general promise in the Scriptures that you may reasonably apply to the particular case before you. If its real meaning includes the particular thing for which you pray, or if you can reasonably apply the principle of the promise to the case, there you have evidence.

For instance, suppose it is a time when wickedness prevails greatly, and you are led to pray for God's interference. What promise have you? Why, this one: "When the enemy shall come in like a flood, the Spirit of the Lord shall lift up a standard against him" (Isaiah 59:19). Here you see a general promise, laying down a principle of God's administration, as a warrant for exercising faith in prayer that you may apply to the case before you. Moreover, if the inquiry is made as to the time in which God will grant blessings in answer to prayer, you have this promise: "While they are yet speaking, I will hear" (Isaiah 65:24).

There are general promises and principles laid down in the Bible which Christians might make use of, if they would only think. Whenever you are in circumstances to which the promises or principles apply, there you are to use them. A parent finds this promise: "The mercy of the Lord is from everlasting to everlasting upon them that fear Him, and His righteousness unto children's children; to such as keep His covenant, and to those that remember His commandments to do them" (Psalm 103:17-18).

Now, here is a promise made to those who possess a certain character. If any parent is conscious that this is his character, he has a rightful ground to apply it to himself and his family. If you are this character, you are bound to make use of this promise in prayer, and believe it, even to your children's children.

I could go from one end of the Bible to the other, and produce an astonishing variety of texts that are applicable as promises. Enough, in fact, to prove that in whatever circumstances a child of God may be placed, God has provided in the Bible some promise, either general or particular, which he can apply, that is precisely suited to his case.

Many of God's promises are very broad, on purpose to cover much ground. What can be broader than the promise in our text: "What things so ever ye desire when ye pray"? What praying Christian is there who has not been surprised at the length and breadth and fullness of the promises of God, when the Spirit has applied them to his heart?

Who that lives a life of prayer has not wondered at his own blindness, in not having before seen and felt the extent of meaning and richness of those promises, when viewed under the light of the Spirit of God? At such times, he has been astonished at his own ignorance, and found the Spirit applying the promises and declarations of the Bible in a sense in which he had never before dreamed of their being applicable.

The manner in which the apostles applied the promises, prophecies, and declarations of the Old Testament, places in a strong light the breadth of meaning, and fullness, and richness of the Word of God. He that walks in the light of God's countenance, and is filled with the Spirit of God as he ought to be, will often make an appropriation of promises that a blind professor of religion would never dream of making. This includes an application of God's promises to his own circumstances and the circumstances of those for whom he prays.

Where there is any prophetic declaration that the thing prayed for is agreeable to the will of God. When it is plain from prophecy that the event is certainly to come, you are bound to believe it, and to make it the ground for your special faith in prayer. If the time is not specified in the Bible, and there is no evidence from other sources, you are not bound to believe that it shall take place now, or immediately.

However, if the time is specified, or if the time may be learned from the study of the prophecies, and it appears to have arrived, then Christians are under obligation to understand and apply it, by offering the prayer of faith. For instance, take the case of Daniel, in regard to the return of the Jews from captivity. What does he say? "I Daniel understood by books the number of the years, whereof the word of the Lord came to Jeremiah the prophet, that He would accomplish seventy years in the desolations of Jerusalem" (Daniel 9:2). Here he learned from books; that is, he studied his Bible, and in that way understood that the length of the captivity was to be seventy years.

What does he do then? Does he sit down upon the promise, and say: "God has pledged Himself to put an end to the captivity in seventy years, and the time has expired, and there is no need of doing anything?" Oh, no.

He says: "And I set my face unto the Lord God, to seek by prayer and supplications, with fasting, and sackcloth, and ashes" (v. 3). He set himself at once to pray that the thing might be accomplished. He prayed in faith. However, what was he to believe? He was to believe what he had learned from the prophecy.

There are many prophecies yet unfulfilled in the Bible that Christians are bound to understand, as far as they are capable of understanding them, and then make them the basis of believing prayer. Do not think, as some seem to do, that because a thing is foretold in prophecy it is not necessary to pray for it, or that it will come whether Christians pray for it or not. God says, in regard to this very class of events, which are revealed in prophecy: "I will yet for this be inquired of by the house of Israel, to do it for them" (Ezekiel 36:37).

When the signs of the times, or the providence of God, indicate that a particular blessing is about to be bestowed, we are bound to believe it. The Lord Jesus Christ blamed the Jews, and called them hypocrites, because they did not understand the indications of Providence. They could understand the signs of the weather and see when it was about to rain, and when it would be fair weather. However, they could not see, from the signs of the times, that the time had come for the Messiah to appear, and build up the house of God.

There are many professors of religion who are always stumbling and hanging back whenever anything is proposed to be done. They always say, "The time has not come, the time has not come." Nevertheless, there are others who pay attention to the signs of the times, and who have spiritual discernment to understand them. These pray in faith for the blessing, and it comes.

When the Spirit of God is upon you, and excites strong desires for any blessing, you are bound to pray for it in faith. You are bound to infer from the fact that you find yourself drawn to desire such a thing while in the exercise of such holy affections as the Spirit of God produces, that these desires are the work of the Spirit. People are not apt to desire with the right kind of desires, unless the Spirit of God excites them.

The apostle refers to these desires, excited by the Spirit, in his Epistle to the Romans, where he says: "Likewise the Spirit also helpeth our infirmities: for we know not what we should pray for as we ought: but the Spirit itself maketh intercession for us with groanings which cannot be uttered. And He that searcheth the hearts knoweth what is the mind of the Spirit, because He maketh intercession for the saints according to the will of God" (Romans 8:26-27).

Here, then, if you find yourself strongly drawn to desire a blessing, you are to understand it as an indication that God is willing to bestow that particular blessing, and so you are bound to believe it. God does not trifle with His children. He does not go and excite in them a desire for one blessing, to turn them off with something else. He excites the very desires He is willing to gratify. Moreover, when they feel such desires, they are bound to follow them until they get the blessing.

4. THIS KIND OF FAITH ALWAYS OBTAINS THE BLESSING SOUGHT.

The text is plain here, to show that you shall receive the very thing for which you have prayed. It does not say: "Believe that ye shall receive, and ye shall either have that or something else equivalent to it." To prove that this faith obtains the very blessing that is asked, I observe:

That otherwise we could never know whether our prayers were answered. We might continue praying and praying, long after the prayer was answered by some other blessing equivalent to the one for which we asked.

If we are not bound to expect the very thing we ask for, it must be that the Spirit of God deceives us. Why should He excite us to desire a certain blessing when He means to grant something else?

What is the meaning of this passage: "If his son ask bread, will he give him a stone?" (Matthew 7:9). Does not our Saviour rebuke the idea that prayer may be answered by giving something else? What encouragement do we have to pray for anything in particular, if we are to ask for one thing and receive another? Suppose a Christian should pray for a revival here and be answered by a revival in China! What if he might pray for a revival and God sends the cholera or an earthquake! All the history of the Church shows that when God answers prayer He gives His people the very thing for which their prayers are offered.

God confers other blessings, on both saints and sinners, which they do not pray for at all. He sends His rain both upon the just and the unjust. Nevertheless, when He answers prayer, it is by doing what they ask Him to do. To be sure, He often goes beyond answering prayer and grants not only what they ask but often connects other blessings with it.

Perhaps a difficulty may be felt about the prayers of Jesus Christ.

People may ask, "Did not He pray in the garden for the cup to be removed, and was His prayer answered?" I answer that this is no difficulty at all, because the prayer was answered. The cup He prayed to be delivered from was removed. This is what the apostle refers to when he says: "Who in the days of His flesh, when He had offered up prayers and supplications with strong crying and tears unto Him that was able to save Him from death, and was heard in that He feared" (Hebrews 5:7).

Some have supposed that He was praying against the cross, and begging to be delivered from dying on the cross! Did Christ ever shrink from the cross? Never. He came into the world on purpose to die on the cross, and He never shrank from it. However, He was afraid He should die in the garden before He came to the cross. The burden on His soul was so great, and produced such an agony that He felt as if He was at the point of dying.

His soul was sorrowful even unto death and the angel appeared unto Him, strengthening Him. He received the very thing for which He asked; as He says: "I knew that Thou hearest Me always" (John 11:42). There is also another case which is often brought up, that of the apostle Paul praying against the "thorn in the flesh."

He says: "I besought the Lord thrice, that it might depart from me." The Lord answered him, "My grace is sufficient for thee"

(2 Corinthians 12:7-9). It is the opinion of Dr. Clarke and others that Paul's prayer was answered in the very thing for which he prayed. "The thorn in the flesh, the messenger of Satan," of which he speaks, was a false apostle who had distracted and perverted the Church at Corinth. Paul prayed against his influence and the Lord answered him by the assurance: "My grace is sufficient for thee."

However, by admitting that Paul's prayer was not answered by the granting of the particular thing for which he prayed, in order to make out this case as an exception to the prayer of faith, they are obliged to assume the very thing to be proved; and that is, that the apostle prayed in faith. There is no reason to suppose that Paul would always pray in faith, any more than that any other Christian does.

The very manner in which God answered him shows that it was not in faith. He virtually tells him, "That thorn is necessary for your sanctification, and to keep you from being exalted above measure. I sent it upon you in love, and in faithfulness, and you have no business to pray that I should take it away. LET IT ALONE."

There is not only no evidence that Paul prayed in faith, but a strong presumption that he did not. From the record, it is evident that he had nothing on which to repose faith. There was no express promise, no general promise that could be applicable, no providence of God, no prophecy, and no teaching of the Spirit that God would remove this thorn. There was, on the other hand, the presumption that God would not remove it, since He had given it for a particular purpose.

The prayer appears to have been selfish, praying against a mere personal influence. This influence was not personal suffering that retarded his usefulness, but, on the contrary, it was given him to increase his usefulness by keeping him humble. However, because on some account, he found it inconvenient and mortifying, he set himself to pray out of his own heart, evidently without being led to do so by the Spirit of God.

Could Paul pray in faith without being led by the Spirit of God, any more than any other man could? In addition, will any one undertake to say that the Spirit of God led him to pray that this might be removed, when God Himself had given it for a particular purpose, which purpose could be answered only as the "thorn" continued with him?

Why, then, is this made an exception to the general rule laid down in the text, that a man shall receive whatsoever he asks in faith? I was once amazed and grieved, at a public examination at a Theological Seminary, to hear them "darken counsel by words without knowledge" on this subject.

This case of Paul, and that of Christ just adverted to, were both cited as instances to prove that the prayer of faith would not be answered in the particular thing for which they prayed. Now, to teach such sentiments as these, in or out of a Theological Seminary, is to trifle with the Word of God, and to break the power of the Christian ministry. Has it come to this, that our grave doctors in our seminaries are employed to instruct Zion's watchmen to believe and teach that it is not to be expected that the prayer of faith is to be answered in the granting of the object for which we pray? Oh, tell it not in Gath, nor let the sound reach Askelon!

What is to become of the Church while such are the views of its gravest and most influential ministers? I would be neither unkind nor censorious, but, as one of the ministers of Jesus Christ, I feel bound to bear testimony against such a perversion of the Word of God.

It is evident that the prayer of faith will obtain the blessing, from the fact that our faith rests on evidence that to grant that thing is the will of God. Not evidence that something else will be granted, but that this particular thing will be. But how, then, can we have evidence that this thing will be granted, if another thing is to be granted? People often receive more than they pray for. Solomon prayed for wisdom, and God granted him riches and honour in addition. Likewise, a wife sometimes prays for the conversion of her husband, and if she offers the prayer of faith, God may not only grant that blessing, but convert her child, and her whole family.

Blessings seem sometimes to "hang together," so that if a Christian gains one he gets them all.

5. HOW WE ARE TO COME INTO THIS STATE OF MIND TO EXERCISE FAITH

That is to say, the state of mind in which we can offer such prayer. People often ask: "How shall I offer such prayer? Shall I say, 'Now I will pray in faith for such and such blessings'?" No, the human mind is not moved in this way. You might just as well say: "Now I will call up a spirit from the bottomless pit."

You must first obtain evidence that God will bestow the blessing. How did Daniel make out to offer the prayer of faith? He searched the Scriptures. Now, you need not let your Bible lie on a shelf, and expect God to reveal His promises to you. "Search the Scriptures," and see where you can get either a general or special promise, or a prophecy, on which you can plant your feet. Go through your Bible, and you will find it full of such precious promises, which you may plead in faith.

A curious case occurred in one of the towns in the western part of the State of New York. There was a revival there. A certain clergyman came to visit the place, and heard a great deal said about the Prayer of Faith. He was staggered at what they said, for he had never regarded the subject in the light in which they did. He inquired about it of the minister that was laboring there.

The minister requested him, in a kind spirit, to go home and take his Testament, look out the passages that refer to prayer, and go round to his most praying people and ask them how they understood these passages. He did so, going to his praying men and women, reading the passages, without note or comment, and asking what they thought.

He found that their plain common sense had led them to understand these passages and to believe that they meant just what they say. This affected him; then, the fact of his presenting the promises before their minds awakened the spirit of prayer in them, and a revival followed.

I could name many individuals who have set themselves to examine the Bible on this subject, who, before they got half through with it, have been filled with the spirit of prayer. They found that God meant by His promises just what a plain, common sense man would understand them to mean. I advise you to try it.

You have Bibles; look them over, and whenever you find a promise that you can use, fasten it in your mind before you go on. You will not get through the Book without finding out that God's promises mean just what they say.

Cherish the good desires you have. Christians very often lose their good desires by not attending to this; and then their prayers are mere words, without any desire or earnestness at all. The least longing of desire must be cherished. If your body were likely to freeze, and you had even the least spark of fire, how you would cherish it! Likewise, if you have the least desire for a blessing, let it be ever so small, do not trifle it away. Do not lose good desires by levity, by censoriousness, by worldly-mindedness. Watch and pray.

Entire consecration to God is indispensable to the prayer of faith. You must live a holy life, and consecrate all to God. This includes your time, talents, influence, all you have and all you are, to be His entirely. Read the lives of pious men, and you will be struck with this fact, that they used to set apart times to renew their covenant, and dedicate themselves anew to God. In addition, whenever they have done so, a blessing has always followed immediately. If I had President Edwards' works here, I could read passages showing how it was in his days.

You must persevere. You are not to pray for a thing once and then cease, and call that the prayer of faith. Look at Daniel. He prayed twenty-one days, and did not cease until he had obtained the blessing. He set his heart and his face unto the Lord, to seek by prayer and supplications, with fasting, and sackcloth, and ashes. He had to hold on for three weeks, and then the answer came.

Why did Daniel's answer not come before? God sent an Archangel to bear the message, but the devil hindered him all this time. See what Christ says in the Parable of the Unjust Judge, and the Parable of the Loaves. What does He teach us by them? Why, that God will grant answers to prayer when it is importunate. "Shall not God avenge His own elect, which cry day and night unto Him?" (Luke 18:7.)

If you would pray in faith, be sure to walk every day with God. If you do, He will tell you what to pray for. Be filled with His Spirit, and He will give you objects enough to pray for. He will give you as much of the spirit of prayer as you have strength of body to bear.

Said a good man to me: "Oh, I am dying for the want of

strength to pray! My body is crushed, the world is on me, and how can I forbear praying?" I have known that man go to bed absolutely sick, for weakness and faintness, under the pressure. And I have known him pray as if he would do violence to Heaven, and then have seen the blessing come as plainly in answer to his prayer as if it were revealed, so that no person would doubt it any more than if God had spoken from heaven.

Shall I tell you how he died? He prayed more and more. He used to take the map of the world before him, and pray, and look over the different countries and pray for them, until he absolutely expired in his room, praying. Blessed man! He was the reproach of the ungodly, and of carnal, unbelieving professors; but he was the favorite of Heaven, and a prevailing prince in prayer.

6. OBJECTIONS BROUGHT AGAINST THIS DOCTRINE

"It leads to fanaticism and amounts to a new revelation." Why should this be a stumbling-block? They must have evidence to believe, before they can offer the prayer of faith. In addition, if God should give other evidence besides the senses, where is the objection?

True, there is a sense in which this is a new revelation; it is making known a thing by His Spirit. However, it is the very revelation that God has promised to give. It is just the one we are to expect, if the Bible is true; that when we know not what we ought to pray for, according to the will of God, His Spirit helps our infirmities, and teaches us. Shall we deny the teaching of the Spirit?

It is often asked, "Is it our duty to offer the prayer of faith for the salvation of all men?" I answer: "No," for that is not a thing according to the will of God. It is directly contrary to His revealed will. We have no evidence that all will be saved. We should feel benevolently to all, and, in itself considered, desire their salvation. Nevertheless, God has revealed that many of the human race shall be damned, and it cannot be a duty to believe that all shall be saved, in the face of a revelation to the contrary. In Christ's prayer in John 17, He expressly said: "I pray not for the world, but for those Thou hast given me" (v. 9).

But some ask, "If we were to offer this prayer for all men, would not all be saved?" I answer, "Yes, and so they would be saved, if they would all repent. But they will not."

But you ask, "For whom are we to pray this prayer? We want to know in what cases, for what persons, and places, and at what times, we are to make the prayer of faith." I answer as I have already answered, "When you have evidence from promises, prophecies, providences, or the leadings of the Spirit, that God will do the things for which you pray."

"How is it that so many prayers of pious parents for their children are not answered? Did you not say there was a promise that pious parents may apply to their children? Why is it, then, that so many pious, praying parents have had impenitent children, who have died in their sins?" Grant that it is so, what does it prove? "Let God be true, but every man a liar" (Romans 3:4). Which shall we believe: that God's promise has failed or that these parents did not do their duty? Perhaps they did not believe the promise or did not believe there was any such thing as the prayer of faith.

Wherever you find a professor who does not believe in any such prayer, you find, as a general thing, that he has children and domestics yet in their sins.

6. Will not these views lead to fanaticism? Will not many

people think they are offering the prayer of faith when they are not?" Unitarians make that same objection against the doctrine of regeneration. They say that many people think they have been born again when they have not. It is an argument against all spiritual religion whatever. Some think they have it when they have not, and are fanatics.

However, there are those who know what the prayer of faith is, just as there are those who know what spiritual experience is, even though it may stumble cold-hearted professors who know it not. Even ministers often lay themselves open to the rebuke that Christ gave to Nicodemus: "Art thou a master in Israel, and knowest not these things?" (John 3:10.)

REMARKS

Persons who have not known by experience what the prayer of faith is, have great reason to doubt their own piety. This is, by no means, uncharitable. Let them examine themselves. The fear is that they understand prayer as little as Nicodemus did the New Birth. They have not walked with God, and you cannot describe it to them, any more than you can describe a beautiful painting to a blind man.

There is reason to believe that millions are in hell because professors have not offered the prayer of faith. When they had promises under their eye, they have not had faith enough to use them. The signs of the times, and the indications of Providence, were favorable, perhaps, and the Spirit of God prompted desires for their salvation. There was evidence enough that God was ready to grant a blessing, and if professors had only prayed in faith, God would have granted it; but He turned it away, because they could not discern the signs of the times.

You say: "This leaves the Church under a great load of guilt." True, it does so; and no doubt multitudes will stand up before God, covered all over with the blood of souls that have been lost through their want of faith. The promises of God, accumulated in their Bibles, will stare them in the face, and weigh them down to hell.

Many professors of religion live so far from God, that to talk to them about the prayer of faith is all unintelligible. Very often the greatest offense possible to them, is to preach about this kind of prayer.

I now want to ask professors a few questions. Do you know what it is to pray in faith? Did you ever pray in this way? Have you ever prayed until your mind was assured the blessing would come or until you felt that rest in God, that confidence, as if you saw God come down from heaven to give it to you? If not, you ought to examine your foundation. How can you live without praying in faith? How do you live in view of your children, while you have no assurance whatever that they will be converted?

One would think you would go deranged. I knew a father who was a good man, but had erroneous views respecting the prayer of faith; and his whole family of children was grown up, without one of them being converted. At length his son sickened, and seemed about to die. The father prayed, but the son grew worse, and seemed sinking into the grave without hope. The father prayed, until his anguish was unutterable.

He went at last and prayed (there seemed no prospect of his son surviving) so that he poured out his soul as if he would not be denied. At length he got an assurance that his son would not only live but be converted; and that not only this one, but his whole family would be converted to God. He came into the house, and told his family his son would not die. They were astonished at him. "I tell you," said he, "he will not die. And no child of mine will ever die in his sins." That man's children were all converted, years ago.

What do you think of that? Was that fanaticism? If you believe so, it is because you know nothing about the matter. Do you pray so? Do you live in such a manner that you can offer such prayer for your children? I know that the children of professors may sometimes be converted in answer to the prayers of somebody else. However, ought you to live so? Dare you trust to the prayers of others, when God calls you to sustain this important relation to your children?

Finally, see what combined effort is made to dispose of the Bible. The wicked are for throwing away the threatenings of the Bible, and the Church the promises. What is there left? Between them, they leave the Bible a blank. I ask in love, "What is our Bible good for, if we do not lay hold of its precious promises, and use them as the ground of our faith when we pray for the blessing of God?"

You had better send your Bibles to the heathen, where they will do some good, if you are not going to believe and use them. I have no evidence that there is much of this prayer now in this Church, or in this city. What will become of them? What will become of your children, your neighbors, the wicked?

6

THE SPIRIT OF PRAYER

"Likewise the Spirit also helpeth our infirmities: for we know not what we should pray for as we ought: but the Spirit itself maketh intercession for us with groanings which cannot be uttered. And He that searcheth the hearts knoweth what is the mind of the Spirit, because He maketh intercession for the saints according to the will of God."

—Romans 8:26-27

MY LAST LECTURE BUT ONE WAS ON THE SUBJECT OF EFFECTUAL Prayer in which I observed that one of the most important attributes of effectual or prevailing prayer is FAITH. This was so extensive a subject that I reserved it for a separate discussion. Accordingly, my last Lecture was on the subject of Faith in Prayer, or, as it is termed, the Prayer of Faith.

It was my intention to discuss the subject in a single Lecture. But as I was under the necessity of condensing so much on some points, it occurred to me, and was mentioned by others, that there might be some questions that ought to be answered more fully, especially as the subject is one on which there is so much darkness. One grand design in preaching is to exhibit the truth in such a way as to answer the questions that would naturally arise in the minds of those who read the Bible with attention, and who want to know what it means, so that they can put it in practice. In explaining the text, I propose to show:

1. What Spirit is here spoken of: "The Spirit also helpeth our infirmities."

2. What that Spirit does for us.

3. Why He does what the text declares Him to do.

4. How He accomplishes it.

5. The degree in which He influences the minds of those who are under His influence.

6. How His influences are to be distinguished from the influences of evil spirits, or from the suggestions of our own minds.

7. How we are to obtain this agency of the Holy Spirit.

8. Who have a right to expect to enjoy His influences in this matter—or for whom the Spirit does the things spoken of in the text.

1. WHAT SPIRIT IS SPOKEN

Some have supposed that the Spirit spoken of in the text means our own spirit, or in other words, our own mind. However, a little attention to the text will show plainly that this is not the meaning. "The Spirit helpeth our infirmities" would then read,

"Our own spirit helpeth the infirmities of our own spirit," and, "Our own spirit maketh intercession for our own spirit." You can make no sense of it on that supposition. It is evident from the manner in which the text is introduced that the Spirit referred to is the Holy Ghost.

"For if ye live after the flesh, ye shall die: but if ye through the Spirit do mortify the deeds of the body, ye shall live. For as many as are led by the Spirit of God, they are the sons of God. For ye have not received the spirit of bondage again to fear; but ye have received the spirit of adoption, whereby we cry, Abba, Father. The Spirit itself beareth witness with our spirit, that we are the children of God" (Romans 8:13-16). The text is plainly speaking of the same Spirit.

2. WHAT THE SPIRIT DOES

He intercedes for the saints. "He maketh intercession for us," and "helpeth our infirmities," when "we know not what to pray for as we ought." He helps Christians to pray "according to the will of God," or for the things that God desires them to pray for.

3. WHY IS THE HOLY SPIRIT THUS EMPLOYED?

Because of our ignorance. Because we know not what we should pray for as we ought. We are so ignorant both of the will of God, revealed in the Bible, and of His unrevealed will, as we ought to learn it from His providence.

Mankind is vastly ignorant of both the promises and prophecies of the Bible, and blind to the providence of God. In addition, they are even more in the dark about those points of which God has said nothing but through the leadings of His Spirit.

I have named these four sources of evidence on which to ground faith in prayer: promises, prophecies, providences, and the Holy Spirit. When all other means fail of leading us to the knowledge of what we ought to pray for, the Spirit does it.

4. HOW DOES GOD MAKE INTERCESSION?

In what mode does He operate, so as to help our infirmities?

Not by superseding the use of our faculties. It is not by praying for us, while we do nothing. He prays for us by exciting our faculties. Not that He immediately suggests to us words, or guides our language. Instead, He enlightens our minds, and makes the truth take hold of our souls. He leads us to consider the state of the Church, and the condition of sinners around us.

The manner in which He brings the truth before the mind, and keeps it there until it produces its effect, we cannot tell. Nevertheless, we can know that He leads us to a deep consideration of the state of things; and the result of this, both naturally and philosophically, is deep feeling.

When the Spirit brings the truth before a man's mind there is only one way in which he can keep from deep feeling. That is, by turning away his thoughts, and leading his mind to think of other things. When the Spirit of God brings the truth before them, sinners must feel. They feel wrong, as long as they remain impenitent.

In the same way, if a man is a Christian, and the Holy Spirit brings the subject into warm contact with his heart, it is just as impossible he should not feel, as it is that your hand should not feel if you put it into the fire. If the Spirit of God leads a man to dwell on things calculated to excite overpowering feelings regarding the salvation of souls, and he is not excited thereby, it proves that he has no love for souls, nothing of the Spirit of Christ, and knows nothing about Christian experience.

The Spirit makes the Christian feel the value of souls and the guilt and danger of sinners in their present condition. It is amazing how dark and stupid Christians often are about this. Even Christian parents let their children go right down to hell before their eyes, and scarcely seem to exercise a single feeling, or put forth an effort to save them. And why?

Because they are so blind to what hell is, so unbelieving about the Bible, so ignorant of the precious promises that God has made to faithful parents. They grieve the Spirit of God away, and it is in vain to make them pray for their children, while the Spirit of God is away from them.

He leads Christians to understand and apply the promises of Scripture. It is wonderful that in no age have Christians been able fully to apply the promises of Scripture to the events of life, as they go along. This is not because the promises themselves are obscure. However, there has always been a wonderful disposition to overlook the Scriptures, as a source of light respecting the passing events of life.

How astonished the apostles were at Christ's application of so many prophecies to Himself! They seemed to be continually ready to exclaim, "Astonishing! Can it be so? We never understood it before!" Who, that has witnessed the manner in which the apostles, influenced and inspired by the Holy Ghost, applied passages of the Old Testament to Gospel times, has not been amazed at the richness of meaning which they found in the Scriptures? It has been same with many a Christian; while deeply engaged in prayer he has seen that passages of Scripture are appropriate which he never thought of before as having any such application.

I once knew an individual who was in great spiritual darkness. He had retired for prayer, resolved that he would not desist until he had found the Lord. He kneeled down and tried to pray. All was dark, and he could not pray. He rose from his knees, and stood awhile; but he could not give it up, for he had promised that he would not let the sun go down before he had given himself to God. He knelt again; but was all dark, and his heart was as hard as before. He was nearly in despair, and said in agony, "I have grieved the Spirit of God away, and there is no promise for me. I am shut out from the presence of God."

However, he was resolved not to give in and again he knelt down. He had said but a few words when this passage came into his mind, as fresh as if he had just read it: "Ye shall seek Me, and find Me, when ye shall search for Me with all your heart" (Jeremiah 29:13). He saw that though this promise was in the Old Testament, and addressed to the Jews, it was still as applicable to him as to them. This broke his heart, like the hammer of the Lord, in a moment. He prayed, and rose up happy in God.

Thus, it often happens when professors of religion are praying for their children. Sometimes they pray, and are in darkness and doubt, feeling as if there were no foundation for faith, and no special promises for the children of believers. However, while they have been pleading, God has shown them the full meaning of some promise, and their soul has rested on it as on His mighty arm. I once heard of a widow who was greatly exercised about her children, until this passage was brought powerful to her mind: "Thy fatherless children, I will preserve them alive; and let Thy widows trust in me" (Jeremiah 49:11).

She saw it had an extended meaning, and she was empowered to lay hold of it, as it were, with her hands. She prevailed in prayer, and her children were converted. The Holy Spirit was sent into the world by the Saviour to guide His people, and instruct them and bring things to their remembrance, as well as to convince the world of sin.

The Spirit leads Christians to desire and pray for things of which nothing is specifically said in the Word of God. Take the case of an individual. That God is willing to save is a general truth. Therefore, it is a general truth that He is willing to answer prayer. However, how shall I know the will of God respecting that individual, whether I can pray in faith according to the will of God for the conversion and salvation of that individual, or not?

Here the agency of the Spirit comes in to lead the minds of God's people to pray for those individuals at those times when God is prepared to bless them. When we know not what to pray for, the Holy Spirit leads the mind to dwell on some object, to consider its situation, to realize its value, and to feel for it, and pray, and "travail in birth," until the person is converted. This sort of experience, I know, is less common in cities than it is in some parts of the country, because of the infinite number of things that in cities divert the attention and grieve the Spirit.

I have had much opportunity to know how it has been in some districts. I was acquainted with an individual who used to keep a list of persons for whom he was especially concerned. In addition, I have had the opportunity to know a multitude of persons, for whom he became thus interested, who were immediately converted. I have seen him pray for persons on his list when he was literally in an agony for them; and have sometimes known him to call on some other person to help him pray for such a one. I have known his mind to fasten thus on an individual of hardened, abandoned character, and who could not be reached in any ordinary way.

In a town in a north part of this State, where there was a revival, there was a certain individual who was a most violent and outrageous opposer. He kept a tavern, and used to delight in swearing at a desperate rate, whenever there were Christians within hearing, on purpose to hurt their feelings. He was so bad that one man said he believed he should have to sell his place, or give it away, and move out of town, for he could not live near a man who swore so.

This good man of whom I was speaking passed through the town, and, hearing of the case, was very much grieved and distressed for the individual. He took him on his praying list. The case weighed on his mind when he was asleep and when he was awake. He kept thinking about the ungodly man, and praying for him for days.

The first we knew of it, the tavern keeper came into a meeting, got up and confessed his sins, and poured out his soul. His barroom immediately became the place where they held prayer meetings. In this manner the Spirit of God leads individual Christians to pray for things that they would not pray for, unless the Spirit led them; and thus they pray for things "according to the will of God."

Saying that this kind of influence amounts to a new revelation has done great evil. Many people will be so afraid of it, if they hear it called a new revelation, that they will not stop to inquire what it means, or whether the Scriptures teach it or not. The plain truth of the matter is, that the Spirit leads a man to pray; and if God leads a man to pray for an individual, the inference from the Bible is, that God designs to save that individual. If we find, by comparing our state of mind with the Bible, that we are led by the Spirit to pray for an individual, we have good evidence to believe that God is prepared to bless him.

By giving to Christians a spiritual discernment respecting the movements and developments of Providence. Devoted, praying Christians often see these things so clearly, and look so far ahead, as greatly to offend others. They sometimes almost seem to prophesy. No doubt, persons may be deluded, and sometimes are, by leaning to their own understanding when they think the Spirit leads them.

However, there is no doubt that a Christian may be made to discern clearly the signs of the times, so as to understand, by Providence, what to expect, and thus to pray for it in faith. Thus, they are often led to expect a revival, and to pray for it in faith, when nobody else can see the least signs of it.

There was a woman in New Jersey, in a place where there had been a revival. She was very positive there was going to be another. She wanted to have "conference meetings" appointed. However, the minister and elders saw nothing to encourage it, and would do nothing. She saw they were blind, and so she went forward, and got a carpenter to make seats for her, for she said she would have meetings in her own house; there was certainly going to be a revival. She had scarcely opened her doors for meetings, before the Spirit of God came down with great power, and these sleepy Church members found themselves surrounded all at once with convicted sinners.

They could only say, "Surely the Lord is in this place; and we knew it not" (Genesis 28:16). The reason why such persons as this praying woman understand the indication of God's will is not because of the superior wisdom that is in them, but because the Spirit of God leads them to see the signs of the times. This is not by revelation but they are led to see that converging of providences to a single point that produces in them a confident expectation of a certain result.

5. THE DEGREE OF INFLUENCE

In what degree are we to expect the Spirit of God to affect

the minds of believers? The text says, "The Spirit maketh intercession with groanings that cannot be uttered." The meaning of this I understand to be, that the Spirit excites desires too great to be uttered except by groans. This makes the soul too full to utter its feelings by words, so that the person can only groan them out to God, who understands the language of the heart.

6. DISTINGUISHING THE INFLUENCES

How are we to know whether it is the Spirit of God that influences our minds, or not?

Not by feeling that some external influence or agency is applied to us. We are not to expect to feel our minds in direct physical contact with God.

If such a thing can be, we know of no way in which it can be made sensible. We know that we exercise our minds freely, and that our thoughts are exercised on something that excites our feelings. However, we are not to expect a miracle to be wrought as if we were led by the hand, by our senses, or like something whispered in the ear, or any miraculous manifestation of the will of God.

Individuals often grieve the Spirit away, because they do not harbor Him and cherish His influences. Sinners often do this ignorantly. They suppose that if they were under conviction by the Spirit, they should have such-and-such mysterious feelings. They falsely suppose a shock would come upon them that they could not mistake.

Many Christians are just as ignorant of the Spirit's influences, and have thought so little about having His assistance in prayer, that when they have such influences they do not know it, and so do not yield to them, and cherish them. Our senses are not affected in the case, only the movement of our own minds. There is nothing else that can be felt. We are merely sensible that our thoughts are intensely focused on a certain subject.

Christians are often unnecessarily misled and distressed on this point, for fear they have not the Spirit of God. They feel intensely, but they know not what makes them feel. They are distressed about sinners, and should be distressed when they think of their condition? They keep thinking about them all the time, and why should they not be distressed?

Now the truth is, that the very fact that you are thinking upon them is evidence that the Spirit of God is leading you. Do you not know that the greater part of the time these things do not affect you this way? The greater part of the time, you do not think much about the case of sinners. You know their salvation is always just as important.

Sometimes, even when you are quite at leisure, your mind is entirely dark, and vacant of any feeling for them. However now, although you may be busy about other things, you think, pray and feel intensely for them, even while you are about business that at other times would occupy all your thoughts. Now, almost every thought you have is, "God have mercy upon them!" Why is this?

Why, their case is placed in a strong light before your mind. Do you ask what it is that leads your mind to exercise benevolent feelings for sinners, and to agonize in prayer for them? What can it be but the Spirit of God?

There are no devils that would lead you this way. If your feelings are truly benevolent, you are to consider it as the Holy Spirit leading you to pray for things according to the will of God.

If we feel any mercy / compassion / yearning for sinners' salvation, it is the Holy Spirit's influence. Don't doubt it!

137

"Try the spirits" by the Bible. People are sometimes led away by strange fantasies and crazy impulses. If you compare them faithfully with the Bible, you never need to be led astray. You can always know whether your feelings are produced by the Spirit's influences, by comparing your desires with the spirit and temper of religion, as described in the Bible.

The Bible commands you to "try the spirits." "Beloved, believe not every spirit, but try the spirits whether they are of God" (1 John 4:1).

7. HOW SHALL WE OBTAIN THIS AGENCY OF THE HOLY SPIRIT?

It must be sought by fervent, believing prayer. Christ says, "If ye then, being evil, know how to give good gifts unto your children; how much more shall your heavenly Father give the Holy Spirit to them that ask Him?" (Luke 11:13).

Does any one say, I have prayed for it, and it does not come? It is because you do not pray aright. "Ye ask, and receive not, because ye ask amiss, that ye may consume it upon your lusts" (James 4:3). You do not pray from right motives. A professor of religion, and a principal member in a Church, once asked a minister what he thought of his case. He had been praying week after week for the Spirit, and had not found any benefit. The minister asked what his motive in praying was.

He replied that, "He wanted to be happy." He knew those who had the Spirit were happy, and he wanted to enjoy his mind as they did. Why, the devil himself might pray so! That is mere selfishness. The man, when this was shown him, at first turned away in anger. He saw that he had never known what it was to pray. He was convinced he was a hypocrite, and that his prayers were all selfish, dictated only by a desire for his own happiness.

David prayed that God would uphold him by His free Spirit, that he might teach transgressors and turn sinners to God. A Christian should pray for the Spirit that he might be the more useful and glorify God more; not that he himself may be happier. This man saw clearly where he had been in error, and he was converted. Perhaps many here have been making just the same mistake. You ought to examine and see if your prayers are not stained with selfishness.

Use the means adapted to stir up your minds on the subject, and to keep your attention fixed there. If a man prays for the Spirit, and then diverts his mind to other objects, if he uses no other means, but goes away to worldly objects, he tempts God. He swings loose from his object, and it would be a miracle if he should get what he prays for.

How is a sinner to get conviction? Why, by thinking of his sins. That is the way for a Christian to obtain deep feeling, by thinking upon the object. God is not going to pour these things on you without any effort of your own. You must cherish the slightest impressions.

Take the Bible, and go over the passages that show the condition and prospects of the world. Look at the world, look at your children, and your neighbors, and see their condition while they remain in sin. Then, persevere in prayer and efforts until you obtain the blessing of the Spirit of God to dwell in you. This was the way, doubtless, that Dr. Watts came to have the feelings that he has described in his hymn:

My thoughts on awful subjects dwell, Damnation and the dead; what horrors seize the guilty soul upon a dying bed!

Look, as it were, through a telescope that will bring it up near to you. Look into hell, and hear them groan. Then turn the glass upwards and look into heaven, and see the saints there, in their white robes, with their harps in their hands, and hear them sing the song of redeeming love. Now ask yourself, "Is it possible that I should prevail with God to elevate the sinner there?" Do this, and if you are not a wicked man, and a stranger to God, you will soon have as much of the spirit of prayer as your body can sustain.

You must watch unto prayer. You must keep a lookout, and see if God grants the blessing when you ask Him. People sometimes pray and never look to see if the prayer is granted.

Be careful also, not to grieve the Spirit of God. Confess and forsake your sins. God will never lead you as one of His hidden ones, and let you into His secrets, unless you confess and forsake your sins. Be not always confessing and never forsaking, but confess and forsake too. Make redress wherever you have committed an injury. You cannot expect to get the spirit of prayer first, and repentance afterwards. You cannot fight it through so. Professors of religion, who are proud and unyielding, and justify themselves, never will force God to dwell with them.

4. Aim to obey perfectly the written law. In other words, have no fellowship with sin. Aim at being entirely above the world. "Be ye therefore perfect, even as your Father which is in heaven is perfect" (Matthew 5:48). If you sin at all, let it be your daily grief. The man who does not aim at this, means to live in sin. Such a man need not expect God's blessing, for he is not sincere in desiring to keep all His commandments.

8. FOR WHOM DOES THE SPIRIT INTERCEDE?

The answer is that "He maketh intercession for the saints," for all saints, for any who are saints.

REMARKS

Why do you suppose it is that so little stress is laid on the influences of the Spirit in prayer, when so much is said about His influences in conversion? Many people are amazingly afraid the Spirit's influences will be left out. They lay great stress on the Spirit's influences in converting sinners. However, how little is said, how little is printed, about His influence in prayer! How little complaining there is that people do not make enough of the Spirit's influence in leading Christians to pray according to the will of God!

Let it never be forgotten that no Christian ever prays aright, unless led by the Spirit. He has natural power to pray, and so far as the will of God is revealed, is able to do it; but he never does, unless the Spirit of God influences him; just as sinners are able to repent, but never do, unless influenced by the Spirit.

This subject lays open the foundation of the difficulty felt by many persons on the subject of the Prayer of Faith. They object to the idea that faith in prayer is a belief that we shall receive the very things for which we ask, and insist that there can be no foundation or evidence upon which to rest such a belief.

In a sermon upon this subject a writer brings forward this difficulty, and presents it in its full strength. "I have," says he, "no evidence that the thing prayed for will be granted, until I have prayed in faith; because, praying in faith is the condition upon which it is promised. And, of course, I cannot claim the promise, until I have fulfilled the condition. Now, if the condition is that I am to believe I shall receive the very blessing for which I ask, it is evident that the promise is given upon the performance of an impossible condition, and is, of course, a mere nullity.

The promise would amount to just this: You shall have whatsoever you ask, upon the condition that you first believe that you shall receive it. Now I must fulfill the condition before I can claim the promise, but I can have no evidence that I shall receive it until I have believed that I shall receive it. This reduces me to the necessity of believing that I shall receive it, before I have any evidence that I shall receive it; which is impossible."

The whole force of this objection arises out of the fact that the Spirit's influences are entirely overlooked, which He exerts in leading an individual to the exercise of faith. It has been supposed that the passage in Mark 11:22-24, with other kindred promises on the subject of the Prayer of Faith, relate exclusively to miracles. Suppose this were true. I would ask, "What were the apostles to believe, when they prayed for a miracle?"

Were they to believe that the precise miracle would be performed for which they prayed? It is evident that they were. In the verses just alluded to, Christ says, "For verily I say unto you, that whosoever shall say unto this mountain, Be thou removed, and be thou cast into the sea; and shall not doubt in his heart, but shall believe that those things which he saith shall come to pass; he shall have whatsoever he saith. Therefore I say unto you, What things soever ye desire when ye pray, believe that ye receive them, and ye shall have them." Here it is evident, that the thing to be believed, and which they were not to doubt in their heart, was that they should have the very blessing for which they prayed.

Now the objection above stated, lies in all its force against this kind of faith, when praying for the performance of a miracle. If it is impossible to believe this in praying for any other blessing, it was equally so in praying for a miracle. I might ask, "Could an apostle believe that the miracle would be wrought, before he had fulfilled the condition, inasmuch as the condition was, that he should believe that he should receive that for which he prayed?" Either the promise is a nullity and a deception, or there is a possibility of performing the condition.

Now, as I have said, the whole difficulty lies in the fact that the Spirit's influences are entirely overlooked, and that faith which is of the operation of God, is left out of the question. If the objection is good against praying for any object, it is as good against praying in faith for the performance of a miracle. The fact is, that the Spirit of God could give evidence, on which to believe that any particular miracle would be granted; could lead the mind to a firm reliance upon God, and trust that the blessing sought would be obtained. And so at the present day He can give the same assurance, in praying for any blessing that we need.

Praying is the same thing, whether you pray for the conversion of a soul, or for a miracle. Faith is the same thing in the one case as in the other. It only terminates on a different object. In one case, it terminates on the conversion of a soul, and in the other on the performance of a miracle.

Nor is faith exercised in one more than the other without reference to a promise, and a general promise may with the same propriety be applied to the conversion of a soul as to the performance of a miracle. In addition, it is equally true in the one case as the other, that no man ever prays in faith without being influenced by the Spirit of God. And if the Spirit could lead the mind of an apostle to exercise faith in regard to a miracle, He can lead the mind of another Christian to exercise faith in regard to receiving any other blessing, by a reference to the same general promise.

Should any one ask: "When are we under an obligation to believe that we shall receive the blessing for which we ask?" I answer:

A. When there is a particular promise, specifying the

particular blessing: as where we pray for the Holy Spirit.
This blessing is particularly named in the promise, here we have
evidence, and we are required to believe, whether we have any
Divine influence or not. Just as sinners are required to repent
whether the Spirit strives with them or not, their obligation rests
not upon the Spirit's influences, but upon the powers of moral
agency that they possess, and upon their ability to do their duty.

While it is true that not one of them ever will repent without the
influences of the Spirit, still they have power to do so, and are under
obligation to do so whether the Spirit strives with them or not. This
works the same for the Christian. He is required to believe where he
has evidence. Although he never does believe, even where he has
an express promise, without the Spirit of God, yet his obligation to
do so rests upon his ability, and not upon the Divine influence.

**B. Where God makes a revelation by His providence, we
are bound to believe in proportion to the clearness of the providential indication.** Therefore, where there is a prophecy, we are
bound also to believe. However, in neither of these cases do we, in
fact, believe, without the Spirit of God.

Where there is neither promise, providence, nor prophecy, on
which we are to repose our faith, we are under no obligation to
believe, unless, as I have shown in this discourse, the Spirit gives
us evidence, by creating desires, and by leading us to pray for a
particular object. In the case of those promises of a general nature,
where we are honestly at a loss to know in what particular cases to
apply them, it may be considered as our privilege rather than our
duty, in many instances, to apply them to particular cases.

Whenever the Spirit of God leads us to apply these promises
to a particular object, then it becomes our duty so to apply them.
In this case, God explains His own promise, and shows how He
designed it should be applied. Our obligation, then, to make this

application, and to believe in reference to this particular object, remains in full force.

C. Some have supposed that Paul prayed in faith for the removal of the thorn in the flesh, and that it was not granted. However, they cannot prove that Paul prayed in faith. The presumption is all on the other side, as I have shown in a former lecture. He had neither promise, nor prophecy, nor providence, nor the Spirit of God, to lead him to believe. The whole objection goes on the ground that the apostle might pray in faith without being led by the Spirit.

This is truly a short method of disposing of the Spirit's influences in prayer. Certainly, to assume that he prayed in faith is to assume, either that he prayed in faith without being led by the Spirit or that the Spirit of God led him to pray for that which was not according to the will of God.

I have dwelt the more on this subject, because I want to have it made so plain that you will be careful not to grieve the Spirit. I want you to have high ideas of the Holy Ghost, and to feel that nothing good will be done without His influences. No praying or preaching will be of any avail without Him. If Jesus Christ were to come down here and preach to sinners, not one would be converted without the Spirit. Be careful, then, not to grieve Him away, by slighting or neglecting His heavenly influences when He invites you to pray.

D. In praying for an object, it is necessary to persevere till you obtain it. Oh, with what eagerness Christians sometimes pursue a sinner in their prayers, when the Spirit of God has fixed their desires on him! No miser pursues gold with so fixed a determination.

E. The fear of being led by impulses has done great injury,

by not being duly considered. A person's mind may be led by an *ignis fatuus*. However, we do wrong if we let the fear of impulses lead us to resist the good impulses of the Holy Ghost. No wonder Christians have not the spirit of prayer if they are unwilling to take the trouble to distinguish; but will reject or resist all impulses, and all leadings of invisible agents.

A great deal has been said on the subject of fanaticism, that is very unguarded, and that causes many minds to reject the leadings of the Spirit of God. "As many as are led by the Spirit of God, they are the sons of God" (Romans 8:14). In addition, it is our duty to "try the spirits whether they are of God" (1 John 4:1). We should insist on close scrutiny, and an accurate discrimination. There must be such a thing as being led by the Spirit, and when we are convinced it is of God, we should be sure to follow. We must follow on, with full confidence that He will not lead us wrong.

F. We see from this subject the absurdity of using set forms of prayer. The very idea of using a form rejects, of course, the leadings of the Spirit. Nothing is more calculated to destroy the spirit of prayer, and entirely to darken and confuse the mind, as to what constitutes prayer, than to use forms. Forms of prayer are not only absurd in themselves, but they are the very device of the devil to destroy the spirit and break the power of prayer. It is of no use to say the form is a good one.

Prayer does not consist in words. It matters not what the words are if the heart is not led by the Spirit of God. If the desire is not enkindled, the thoughts directed, and the whole current of feeling produced and led by the Spirit of God, it is not prayer. Set forms are, of all things, best calculated to keep an individual from praying as he ought.

G. The subject furnishes a test of character. "The Spirit maketh intercession," for whom? For the saints. Those who are saints are thus exercised. If you are saints you know by experience what it is to be thus exercised; or, if you do not, it is because you have grieved the Spirit of God so that He will not lead you. You live in such a manner that this Holy Comforter will not dwell with you, nor give you the spirit of prayer.

If this is so, you must repent. Do not stop to settle whether you are a Christian or not, but repent, as if you never had repented. Do your first works. I do not take it for granted that you are a Christian, but go, like a humble sinner, and pour out your heart unto the Lord. You never can have the spirit of prayer in any other way.

H. It is important to understand this subject:

(1.) In order to be useful. Without this spirit, there can be no such sympathy between God and you so that you can either walk with God or work with God. You need to have a strong beating of your heart with His, or you need not expect to be greatly useful.

(2.) As being important to your sanctification. Without such a spirit you will not be sanctified, nor will you understand the Bible, and therefore you will not know how to apply it to your case. I want you to feel the importance of having God with you all the time. If you live as you ought, He says He will come unto you, and make His abode with you, and sup with you, and you with Him.

I. If people know not the spirit of prayer, they are very apt to be unbelieving in regard to the results of prayer. They do not see what takes place, do not see the connection, or do not see the evidence. They are not expecting spiritual blessings. When sinners are convicted, they conclude that such are merely frightened by terrible preaching. When people are converted, they feel no confidence, saying, "We will see how they turn out."

J. Those who have the spirit of prayer know when the blessing comes. It was just the same when Jesus Christ appeared. Those ungodly doctors did not know Him. Why? Because they were not praying for the redemption of Israel. However, Simeon and Anna knew Him. How was that? Mark what they said, how they prayed, and how they lived. They were praying in faith, and so they were not surprised when He came (Luke 2:25-38).

Therefore, it is the same with the Christians of whom I speak. If sinners are convicted or converted, they are not surprised at it. They are expecting just such things. They know God when He comes, because they are looking out for His visits.

K. There are three classes of persons in the Church who are liable to error, or have left the truth out of view, on this subject.

(1.) Those who place great reliance on prayer, and use no other means. They are alarmed at any special means, and talk about your "getting up a revival."

(2.) Over against these are those who use means, and pray, but never think about the influences of the Spirit in prayer. They talk about prayer for the Spirit, and feel the importance of the Spirit in the conversion of sinners, but do not realize the importance of the Spirit in prayer. Their prayers are all cold talk, nothing that anybody can feel, or that can take hold of God.

(3.) Those who have certain strange notions about the Sovereignty of God, and are waiting for God to convert the world without prayer or means.

There must be in the Church a deeper sense of the need of the spirit of prayer. The fact is, that, generally, those who use means most assiduously, and make the most strenuous efforts for the salvation of men, and who have the most correct notions of the manner in which means should be used for converting sinners, also pray most for the Spirit of God, and wrestle most with God for His blessing. What is the result?

Let the facts speak and determine whether these persons do or do not pray, and whether the Spirit of God does not testify to their prayers, and follow their labors with His power.

L. Nothing will produce an excitement and opposition so quickly as the spirit of prayer. If any person should feel burdened with the case of sinners, so as to groan in his prayer, some become nervous, and he is visited at once with rebuke and opposition! From my soul, I abhor all affectation of feeling where none exists, and all attempts to work one's self up into feeling, by groans. However, I feel bound to defend the position, that there is such a thing as being in a state of mind in which there is but one way to keep from groaning; and that is, by resisting the Holy Ghost.

I was once present where this subject was discussed. It was said, "Groaning ought to be discountenanced." The question was asked in reply, whether God cannot produce such a state of feeling, that to abstain from groaning is impossible. The answer was, "Yes, but He never does." Then the apostle Paul was egregiously deceived when he wrote about groanings that cannot be uttered and Edwards was deceived when he wrote his book upon revivals.

Revivals are all in the dark. Now, no man who reviews the history of the Church will adopt such a sentiment. I do not like this attempt to shut out, or stifle, or keep down, or limit, the spirit of prayer. I would sooner cut off my right hand than rebuke the spirit of prayer, as I have heard of its being done by saying, "Do not let me hear any more groaning!"

I hardly know where to end this subject. I should like to discuss it a month, indeed, until the whole Church could understand it, to pray the prayer of faith. Beloved, I want to ask you: Do you believe all this? Do you wonder that I should talk so? Perhaps some of you have had some glimpses of these things. Now, will you give yourselves up to prayer, and live to have the spirit of prayer, and have the Spirit with you all the time? Oh, for a praying Church!

I once knew a minister who had a revival fourteen winters in succession. I did not know how to account for it, until I saw one of his members get up in a prayer meeting and make a confession. "Brethren," said he, "I have been long in the habit of praying every Saturday night till after midnight, for the descent of the Holy Ghost among us. And now, brethren," and he began to weep, "I confess that I have neglected it for two or three weeks." The secret was out. That minister had a praying Church.

Brethren, in my present state of health, I find it impossible to pray as much as I have been in the habit of doing, and yet continue to preach. It overcomes my strength. Now, shall I give myself up to prayer, and stop preaching? That will not do. Now, will not you, who are in health, throw yourselves into this work, and bear this burden, and give yourselves to prayer, until God shall pour out His blessing upon us?

a prayful Church

7

AN APPROVING HEART— CONFIDENCE IN PRAYER

From: *The Oberlin Evangelist*
March 3, 1847

> *"Beloved, if our heart condemn us not, then have we confidence toward God. And whatever we ask, we receive of him, because we keep his commandments, and do those things that are pleasing in his sight."*
> —1 John 3:21-22

In resuming and pursuing this subject, I shall,

I. Show that if our heart does not condemn us, we have and cannot but have confidence toward God that He accepts us

II. That if we have confidence that our heart does not condemn us, we shall also have confidence that God will grant us what we ask

III. Show why this is so, and why we know it to be so.

I. OUR HEART DOES NOT CONDEMN US.

If our heart really does not condemn us, it is because we are conscious of being conformed to all the light we have, and of doing the whole will of God as far as we know it. While in this state it is impossible that with right views of God's character, we should conceive of Him as condemning us. Our intelligence instantly rejects the supposition that He does or can condemn us, that is for our present state.

We may be most deeply conscious that we have done wrong heretofore, and we may feel ourselves to be most guilty for this, and may be sure that God disapproves those past sins of ours, and would condemn us for them even now, if the pardoning blood of Christ had not intervened. But where pardon for past sins has been sought and found through redeeming blood, "there is therefore no more condemnation" for the past.

In reference to the present, the obvious truth is that if our conscience fully approves of our state, and we are conscious of having acted according to the best light we have, it contradicts all our just ideas of God to suppose that He condemns us. He is a father, and He cannot but smile on His obedient and trusting children.

Indeed, ourselves being in this state of mind, it is impossible for us not to suppose that God is well pleased with our present state. We cannot conceive of Him as being otherwise than pleased; for if He were displeased with a state of sincere and full obedience, He would act contrary to His own character; He would cease to be benevolent, holy, and just. We cannot therefore conceive of Him as refusing to accept us when we are conscious of obeying His will so far as we know it. Suppose the case of a soul appearing before God, fully conscious of seeking with all the heart to please

God. In this case the soul must see that this is such a state as must please God.

Let us turn this subject over till we get it fully before our minds. For what is it that our conscience rightly condemns us? Plainly for not obeying God according to the best light we have. Suppose now we turn about and fully obey the dictates of conscience. Then its voice approves and ceases to condemn. Now all just views of the Deity require us to consider the voice of conscience in both cases as only the echo of His own. The God who condemns all disobedience must of necessity approve of obedience, and to conceive of Him as disapproving our present state would be in the conviction of our own minds to condemn Him.

It is therefore by no means presumption in us to assume that God accepts those who are conscious of really seeking supremely to please and obey Him.

Again let it be noted that in this state with an approving conscience, we should have no self-righteousness. A man in this state would at this very moment ascribe all his obedience to the grace of God. From his inmost soul he would say, "By the grace of God, I am what I am." And nothing could be further from his heart than to take praise or glory to himself for anything good.

Yet I have sometimes been exceedingly astonished to hear men and even ministers of the gospel speak with surprise and incredulity of such a state as our text presupposes—a state in which a man's conscience universally approves of his moral state. But why be incredulous about such a state? Or why deem it a self-righteous and sinful state! A man in this state is as far as can be from ascribing glory to himself. No state can be further from self-righteousness. So far is this from being a self-righteous state, the fact is that every other state but this is self-righteous, and this alone is exempt from that sin. Mark how the man in this state ascribes all to the grace of

God.

The apostle Paul, when in this state of conscious uprightness, most heartily ascribes all to grace. He says, "I laboured more abundantly than they all, yet not I, but the grace of God that is in me."

But, observe that while the apostle was in that state, it was impossible that he should conceive of God as displeased with his state. Paul might greatly and justly condemn himself for his past life, and might feel assured that God disapproved and had condemned Saul, the proud persecutor, though he had since pardoned Saul, the praying penitent. But the moral state of Paul, the believer; of Paul, the untiring labourer for Christ; of Paul whose whole heart and life divine grace has now moulded into its own image. This moral state Paul's conscience approves, and his views of God compel him to believe that God approves.

So of the apostle John. Hear what he says. "Whatsoever we ask, we receive of him, because we keep his commandments and do those things that are pleasing in his sight."

But here rises up a man to rebuke the apostle. "What?" he says. "Did you not know that your heart is corrupt, that you never can know all its latent wickedness, that you ought never to be so presumptuous as to suppose that you 'do those things that please God?' Did you not know that no mere man does ever, even by any grace received in this life, really 'keep the commandments of God so as to do those things that are pleasing in His sight?'"

"No," says John. "I did not know that."

"What?" rejoins his reprover. "Not know that sin is mixed with all you do, and that the least sin is displeasing to God!"

"Indeed," replies John. "I knew I was sincerely trying to please God, and verily supposed I did please Him and did keep His commandments, and that it was entirely proper to say so—all to the praise of upholding, sanctifying grace."

Again, when a man prays disinterestedly, and with a heart in full and deep sympathy with God, he may and should have confidence that God hears him. When he can say in all honesty before the Lord, "Now, Lord, thou knowest that through the grace of thy Spirit my soul is set on doing good to men for thy glory. I am grieved for the dishonour done to Thee, so that rivers of water run down my eyes, because men keep not thy law," then he knows that his prayers are acceptable to God.

PRAYING IN SYMPATHY WITH GOD

Indeed no one, having right views of God's character, can come to Him in prayer in a disinterested state of mind, and feel otherwise than that God accepts such a state of mind. Now since our heart cannot condemn us when we are in a disinterested state of mind, but must condemn any other state, it follows that if our heart does not condemn us, we shall have confidence that God hears our prayers and accepts our state as pleasing in His sight.

Again, when we are conscious of sympathizing with God Himself, we may know that God will answer our prayers. There never was a prayer made in this state of sympathy with God, which He failed to answer. God cannot fail to answer such a prayer without denying Himself. The soul, being in sympathy with God, feels as God feels; so that for God to deny its prayers, is to deny His own feelings, and refuse to do the very thing He Himself desires. Since God cannot do this, He cannot fail of hearing the prayer that is in sympathy with His own heart.

In the state we are now considering, the Christian is conscious of praying in the Spirit, and therefore must know that his prayer is accepted before God. I say, he is conscious of this fact. Do not some of you know this? Ye who thus live and walk with God, do you not know that the Spirit of God helps your infirmities and makes intercession for you according to the will of God? Are you not very conscious of these intercessions made for you, and in your very soul as it were, with groanings that cannot be uttered? Your heart within pants and cries out after God, and is lifted up continually before Him as spontaneously as it is when your heart sings, pouring out its deep outgushings of praise. You know how sometimes your heart sings, though your lips move not and you utter no sound. Yet your heart is full of music, making melody to the Lord. Even so, your soul is sometimes in the mood of spontaneous prayer, and pours out its deep-felt supplications into the ears of the Lord of Hosts just as naturally as you breathe. The silent and ceaseless echoing of your heart is, *Thy kingdom come—Thy kingdom come*; and although you may not utter these words, and perhaps not any words at all, yet these words are a fair expression of the overflowing desires of your heart.

And this deep praying of the heart goes on while the Christian is still pursuing the common vocations of life. The man perhaps is behind the counter, or in his workshop planing wood, but his heart is communing or interceding with God. You may see him behind his plow, but his heart is deeply engrossed with his Maker. He follows on, and only now and then, starts up from the intense working of his mind and finds that his land is almost finished. The student has his book open to his lesson, but his deep musings upon God. Or the irrepressible longings of his soul in prayer consume his mental energies, and his eye floats unconsciously over the unnoticed page. God fills his thoughts. He is more conscious of this deep communion with God than he is of the external world. The team he is driving or the book he professes to study is by no means so really and so vividly a matter of conscious recognition to him as is his communion of soul with his God.

In this state the soul is fully conscious of being perfectly submissive to God. Whether he uses these words or not, his heart would always say, "Not my will, O Lord, but thine be done." Hence he knows that God will grant the blessing he asks, if He can do so without a greater evil to His kingdom than the resulting good of bestowing it. We cannot but know that the Lord delights to answer the prayers of a submissive child of His own.

GOD HEARS OUR PRAYERS

Again, when the conscience sweetly and humbly approves, it seems impossible that we should feel so ashamed and confounded before God as to think that He cannot hear our prayer. The fact is, it is only those whose hearts condemn them who come before God ashamed and confounded, and who cannot expect God to answer their prayers. These persons cannot expect to feel otherwise than confounded, until the sting of conscious guilt is taken away by repentance and faith in a Redeemer's blood.

Yet again, the soul in this state is not afraid to come with humble boldness to the throne, as God invites him to do, for he recognizes God as a real and most gracious father, and sees in Jesus a most compassionate and condescending high Priest. Of course, he can look upon God only as being always ready to receive and welcome himself to His presence.

Nor is this a self-righteous state of mind. O, how often have I been amazed and agonized to hear it so represented! But how strange is this! Because you are conscious of being entirely honest before God, therefore it is maintained that you are self-righteous! You ascribe every good thing in yourself most heartily to Divine Grace, but yet you are (so some say) very self-righteous notwithstanding! How long will it take some people to learn what real self-righteousness is? Surely it does not consist in being full of the love and Spirit of God; nor does humility consist in being actually so full of sin and self-condemnation that you cannot feel otherwise than ashamed and confounded before both God and man.

II. WE SHALL RECEIVE THE THINGS WE ASK.

If our heart does not condenm us, we may have confidence that we shall receive the things we ask.

A. This must be so, because it is His Spirit working in us that excites these prayers. God Himself prepares the heart to pray. The Spirit of Christ leads this Christian to the throne of grace and keeps him there; then presents the objects of prayer, enkindles desire, draws the soul into deep sympathy with God. Now, with all this being wrought by the grace and Spirit of God, will He not answer these prayers? Indeed He will. How can He ever fail to answer them?

B. It is a remarkable fact that all real prayer seems to be summed up in the Lord's prayer, and especially in those two most comprehensive petitions—"Thy kingdom come; thy will be done on earth as it is in heaven." The mind in a praying frame runs right into these two petitions, and seems to center here continually. Many other and various things may be specified; but they are all only parts and branches of this one great blessing: Let God's kingdom come, and bear sway on earth as it does in heaven. This is the sum of all true prayer.

Now let it be observed that God desires this result infinitely more than we do. When therefore, we desire it too, we are in harmony with the heart of God, and He cannot deny us. The blessing we crave is the very thing which of all others He most delights to bestow.

C. Yet let it be noted here that God may not answer every

prayer according to its letter; but He surely will according to its spirit. The real spirit is evermore this: "Thy kingdom come—thy will be done." This, God will assuredly answer, because He has so abundantly promised to do this very thing in answer to prayer.

III. WHY WILL GOD CERTAINLY ANSWER SUCH A PRAYER.

A. The text affirms that "whatsoever we ask we receive of Him because we keep His commandments and do those things that are pleasing in His sight." Now we might perhaps understand this to assign our obedience as the reason of God's giving the blessing sought in prayer. But if we should, we should greatly err. The fundamental reason always of God's bestowing blessings is His goodness—His love. Let this be never forgotten. All good flows down from the great fountain of infinite goodness.

Our obedience is only the condition of God's bestowing it—never the fundamental reason or ground of its bestowment. It is very common for us in rather loose and popular language to speak of a condition as being a cause or fundamental reason. But on a point like the present, we ought to use language with more precision. The true meaning on this point undoubtedly is that obedience is the condition. This being fulfilled on our part, the Lord can let His infinite benevolence flow out upon us without restraint. Obedience takes away the obstacle. Then the mighty gushings of Divine Love break forth. Obedience removes the obstacles—never merits, or draws down the blessing.

B. If God were to give blessings upon any other condition, it would deceive multitudes, either respecting ourselves or Himself. If He were to answer our prayers, we being in a wrong state of mind, it would deceive others very probably; for if they did not know us well, they would presume that we were in a right state, and might be led to consider those things in us right which are in fact wrong.

Or, if they knew that we were wrong, and yet knew that God answered our prayers, what must they think of God? They could not avoid the conclusion that He patronizes wrong doing, and lifts up the smiles of His love upon iniquity—and how grievous must be the influence of such conclusions!

It should be borne in mind that God has a character to maintain. His reputation is a good to Himself, and He must maintain it as an indispensable means of sustaining His moral government over other creatures. It could not be benevolent for Him to take a course that would peril His own reputation as a holy God and as a patron and friend of holiness and not of sin.

C. God is well pleased when we remove the obstacles out of the way of His benevolence. He is infinitely good, and lives to do good and for no other purpose—for no other end whatever except to pour forth blessings upon His creatures wherever He can without peril to the well-being of other creatures under His care and love. He exists forever in a state of entire consecration to this end. Such benevolence as this is infinitely right in God, and nothing less than this could be right for Him.

Now, if it is His delight and His life to do good, how greatly must He rejoice when we remove all obstacles out of the way! How does His heart exult when another and yet another opportunity is afforded Him of pouring out blessings in large and rich measure.

Think of it, sinner, for it applies to you! Marvelous as you may think it, and most strange as it may seem—judged of by human rules and human examples, yet of God it cannot fail of being always true that He delights supremely in doing you good, and only waits till you remove the obstacles. Then would His vast love break forth and pour its ocean tides of mercy and of grace all around about you. Go and bow before your injured Sovereign in deep submission and real penitence, with faith also in Jesus for pardon, and thus put this matter to a trial! See if you do not find that His mercies are high above the heavens! See if anything is too great for His love to do for you!

And let each Christian make a similar proof of this amazing love. Place yourself where mercy can reach you without violating the glorious principles of Jehovah's moral government; and then wait and see if you do not experience the most overwhelming demonstrations of His love! How greatly does your Father above delight to pour out His mighty tides of blessings! O, He is never so well pleased as when He finds the channel open and free for these great currents of blessings to flow forth upon His dear people!

A day or two since I received a letter from the man in whose behalf you will recollect that I requested your prayers at a late church prayer meeting. This letter was full of precious interest. The writer has long been a stranger to the blessedness of the gospel; but now he writes me: "I am sure you are praying for me, for within a week I have experienced a peace of mind that is new to me."

I mention this now as another proof of the wonderful readiness of our Father in heaven to hear and answer prayer. O what love is this! To what shall I compare it, and how shall I give you any adequate view of its amazing fullness and strength?

Think of a vast body of water, pent up and suspended high above our heads, pressing and pressing at every crevice to find an outlet where it may gush forth. Suppose the bottom of the vast Pacific should heave and pour its ocean tides over all the continents of the earth. This might illustrate the vast overflowings of the love of God—how grace and love are mounting up far and infinitely above all the mountains of your sins. Yes, let the deep, broad Pacific Ocean be elevated on high and there pent up, and then conceive of its pressure. How it would force its way and pour out its gushing floods wherever the least channel might be opened! And you would not need to fear that your little wants would drain it dry!

O, No! You would understand how there might be enough and to spare—how it might be said, "Open thy mouth wide and I will fill it." The promises might read, "Bring ye all the tithes into my store house, and prove me now herewith, if I will not open you the windows of heaven and pour you out blessings till there be not room enough to receive them." The great oceans of Divine Love are never drained dry. Let Christians but bring in their tithes and make ready their vessels to receive, and then, having fulfilled the conditions, they may "stand still and see the salvation of God."

O how those mountain floods of mercy run over and pour themselves all abroad till every capacity of the soul is filled! O how your little vessels will run over and run over, as in the case of the prophet when the widow's vessels were all full and he cried out—O hasten, hasten—"is there not another vessel?" Still the oil flows on; is there not another vessel? *No more,* she says; *all are full;* then and only then was the flowing oil stayed. How often have I thought of this in seasons of great revival, when Christians really get into a praying frame, and God seems to give them everything they ask for; until at length the prophet cries out, "Is there not yet another vessel? O bring more vessels, more vessels yet, for still the oil is flowing and still runs over." But ah, the church has reached the limit of her expectation. She has provided no more vessels; and the heavenly current is stayed. Infinite love can bless no more; for faith is lacking to prepare for and receive it.

REMARKS

Many persons, being told that God answers prayer for

Christ's sake, overlook the condition of obedience. They have so loose an idea of prayer and of our relations to God in it and of His relations to us and to His moral government that they think they may be disobedient and yet prevail through Christ. How little do they understand the whole subject! Surely they must have quite neglected to study their Bible to learn the truth about prayer. They might very easily have found it there declared, "He that turneth away his ear from hearing the law, even his prayer shall be an abomination." "The sacrifice of the wicked is an abomination to the Lord." "If I regard iniquity in my heart, the Lord will not hear me." All this surely teaches us that if there be the least sin in my heart, the Lord will not hear my prayer.

Nothing short of entire obedience for the time being is the condition of acceptance with God. There must be a sincere and honest heart. How else can you look up with humble confidence and say, "My Father?" How else can you use the name of Jesus as your prevailing Mediator? And how else can God smile upon you before all the eyes of angels and of pure saints above?

When men come before God with their idols set up in their hearts, and the stumbling-block of their iniquity before their faces, the Lord says, "Should they inquire of me at all?" Read and see. Ezekiel 14:3-5. The Lord commissions His prophet to declare unto all such: "I, the Lord, will answer him that cometh thus, according to the multitude of his idols." Such prayers God will answer by sending not a Divine Fullness, but a wasting leanness; not grace and mercy and peace, but barrenness and cursings and death.

Do not some of you know what this is? You have found in your own experience that the more you pray, the harder your heart is. And what do you suppose the reason of this can be? Plainly there can be no other reason for it than this: you come up with the stumbling-block of your iniquity before your face, and God answers you accordingly—not to His great mercies, but to the multitude of your idols.

Should you not take heed how you pray?

Persons never need hesitate because of their past sins, to approach God with the fullest confidence. If they now repent, and are conscious of fully and honestly returning to God with all their heart, they have no reason to fear being repulsed from the footstool of mercy.

I have sometimes heard persons express great astonishment when God heard and answered their prayers, after they had been very great and vile sinners. But such astonishment indicates but little knowledge of the matchless grace and loving kindness of our God. Look at Saul of Tarsus. Once a bitter and mad persecutor, proud in his vain Pharisaism, but now repenting, returning, and forgiven. Mark what power he has with God in prayer. In fact, after penitence, God pardons so fully that, as His word declares, He remembers their iniquities no more. Then the Lord places the pardoned soul on a footing where he can prevail with God as truly and as well as any angel in heaven can! So far as the Bible gives us light on this subject, we must conclude that all this is true. And why? Not because the pardoned Christian is more righteous than an angel; but because he is equally accepted with the purest angel, and has besides the merits and mediation of Jesus Christ, all made available to him when he uses this all-prevalent name.

PRAYING IN JESUS' NAME

Oh, there is a world of meaning in this so-little-thought-of arrangement for prayer in Jesus' name. The value of Christ's merits is all at your disposal. If Jesus Christ could obtain any blessing at the court of heaven, you may obtain the same by asking in His name—it being supposed of course that you fulfill the conditions of acceptable prayer. If you come and pray in the spirit of Christ; His Spirit making intercession with your spirit, and your faith taking hold of His all-meritorious name, you may have His intercessions before the throne in your behalf, and whatever Christ can obtain there, He will obtain for you. "Ask, therefore, now," so Christ Himself invites and promises. "Ask and receive, that your joy may be full."

O, what a vantage ground is this upon which God has placed Christians! O what a foundation on which to stand and plead with most prevailing power! How wonderful! First, God bestows pardon, takes away the sting of death; restores peace of conscience and joy in believing; then gives the benefit of Christ's intercession; and then invites Christians to ask what they will! O, how mighty! How prevalent might every Christian become in prayer! Doubtless we may say that a church living with God, and fully meeting the conditions of acceptable prayer might have more power with God than so many angels. And shall we hear professed Christians talk of having no power with God! Alas, alas! Surely such surely know not their blessed birthright. They have not yet begun to know the gospel of the Son of God!

Many continue the forms of prayer when they are living in sin, and do not try to reform, and even have no sincere desire to reform. All such persons should know that they grievously provoke the Lord to answer their prayers with fearful judgments.

It is only those who live and walk with God whose prayers are of any avail to themselves, to the church, or to the world. Only those whose consciences do not condemn them, and who live in a state of conscious acceptance with God. They can pray. According to our text they receive whatever they ask because they keep His commandments and do the things that are pleasing in His sight.

When those who have been the greatest sinners will turn to God, they may prevail as really as if they had never sinned at all.

When God forgives through the blood of Jesus, it is real forgiveness and the pardoned penitent is welcomed as a child to the bosom of infinite love. For Jesus' sake God receives him without the least danger of its being inferred that Himself cares not for sin. Oh, He told the Universe once and for all how utterly He hated sin. He made this point known when He caused His well-beloved Son to bear our sins in His own body on the tree, and it pleased the Father to bruise Him and hide His face from even the Son of His love. O, what a beautiful, glorious thing this gospel system is! In it God has made such manifestations of His regard for His law that now He has nothing to fear in showing favour to any and every sinner who believes in Christ. If this believing sinner will also put away his sin, if he will only say, "In the name of the Lord I put them all away—all—now—forever," let him do this with all his heart, and God will not fear to embrace him as a son. This penitent needs fear nothing so long as he hides himself in the open cleft of this blessed Rock of Ages.

Look at the case of the prodigal son. Famished, ragged, poor, ready to perish, he remembers his father's house and the plenty that abounds there; he comes to himself and hence looks upon things once more according to their reality. Now he says, "In my father's house there is bread enough and to spare, but here I am perishing with hunger." But why is he ready to perish with hunger? Ah, he ran away from a bountiful and kind father, and spent all his substance in riotous living. But he comes to himself. There, see him drawing near his father's mansion—once his own dear home. See, the father rushes to embrace him; he hastens to make this penitent son most welcome to his home and to his heart. So God makes haste to show that He is not afraid to make the vilest sinner welcome if he only comes back a penitent and rests on the name of Jesus. O what a welcome is this!

Follow on that beautiful illustration of it that the Saviour has given us. Bring forth the best robe. Invite together all our friends and neighbours. Prepare the music. Spread the table, and kill the fatted calf. It is fit that we should make merry and be glad. Lead forward this long-lost son and put on him my best robe. Let there be joy throughout my house over my returned and penitent son.

And what does all this show? One thing—that there is joy in the presence of the angels of God, and joy in the very heart of God Himself over one sinner that repenteth. O, I wonder sinners will not come home to their Father in heaven!

Sinner, if you will come back to the Lord, you may not only prevail for yourself, but for your associates and friends. I was once in a revival where a large company of young men banded themselves together under a mutual pledge that they would not be converted. Father Nash was with me in that revival season, and on one occasion while the young men, too, were all present, he made a declaration that startled me and almost shocked himself. Yet, as he said afterward, he dared not take it back, for he did not know how he came to say it, and perhaps the hand of God might be in it. "Young men," said he. "God will break your ranks within one week, or He will send some of you to hell."

It was an awful time. We feared that possibly it might not prove to be so, and that then the result would be exceeding bad upon the minds of that already hardened band. But it was spoken, and we could only cry unto God.

Time rolled along. About two or three days after this declaration was made, the leader of this band called to see me, all broken down and as mellow as he could be. As soon as he saw me, he cried out, "What shall I do?"

"What are you thinking about?" said I.

"About my wicked companions," said he. "All of them in the way to hell."

"Do you pray for them?" I asked.

"Oh, yes," said he. "I cannot help praying for them every moment."

"Well, then," said I, "there is one thing more; go to them and entreat them in Christ's name to be reconciled to God."

He darted out of my room and began this work in earnest. Suffice it to say, that before the week was closed almost all of that band of young men were converted.

And now let me say to the impenitent sinners in this assembly. If others do not labour to promote a revival, begin at once and do it yourself. Learn from such a case as I have just stated, what you can do. Don't you think you could do something of the greatest value to souls if you would seriously try? Who is there here—let me see—what young man or young woman is there here now impenitent? Do not you believe that if you would repent yourself, you might then go and pray and labour and secure the conversion of others, perhaps many others of your companions?

Sinners are usually disposed to throw all the responsibility of this labour and prayer upon Christians. I throw it back upon you. Do right yourselves and then you can pray. Do right, and then none can labour with more effect than yourselves in this great work of bringing back wandering prodigals to their father's house.

Christian hearer, is it not a dreadful thing for you to be in a state in which you cannot prevail with God? Let us look around. How is it with you? Can you prevail with God; and you—and you? Who are they and how many are there in such a state that their prayers avail nothing, and who know before they pray and while they are praying that they are in no fit state to offer prevailing prayer? One of the brethren, you recollect said to us at a recent church meeting, "I have lost my power to prevail with God. I know I am not ready for this work." How many others are there, still in the same awful condition?

O how many have we here who are the salt of the earth, whose prayers and redeeming influence save the community from becoming perfectly putrid with moral corruption? I hope they will be found alive and at work in this trying hour. O we must have your prayers for the impenitent—for the anxious—for backsliders. Or if you cannot pray, at least come together and confess your sins. Tell your brethren and sisters you cannot pray and beg of them to pray for you that you may be brought back to the light and the peace and the penitence of real salvation.

8

ON PRAYER

From: *The Oberlin Evangelist*
January 3, 1855

> "He spake a parable unto them to this end, that men ought always to pray, and not to faint."
>
> —Luke 18:1

In discussing the subject of prayer, presented in our text, I propose to inquire:

I. Why men should pray at all

II. Why men should pray always and not faint

III. Why men do not pray always

IV. Remarks

I. WHY MEN SHOULD PRAY AT ALL

Our dependence on God is universal, extending to all things. This fact is known and acknowledged. None but atheists presume to call it in question.

Prayer is the dictate of our nature. By the voice of nature this duty is revealed as plainly as possible. We feel the pressure of our wants, and our instincts cry out to a higher power for relief in their supply. You may see this in the case of the most wicked man, as well as in the case of good men. The wicked, when in distress, cry out to God for help. Indeed, mankind has given evidence of this in all ages and in every nation—showing both the universal necessity of prayer, and that it is a dictate of our nature to look up to a God above.

It is a primitive conviction of our minds that God does hear and answer prayer. If men did not assume this to be the case, why should they pray? The fact that men do spontaneously pray shows that they really expect God to hear prayer. It is contrary to all our original belief to assume that events occur under some law of concatenation, too rigid for the Almighty to break, and which He never attempts to adjust according to His will. Men do not naturally believe any such thing as this.

GOD, UNCHANGING

The objection to prayer that God is unchangeable, and therefore cannot turn aside to hear prayer, is altogether a fallacy and the result of ignorance. Consider what is the true idea of God's unchangeableness. Surely, it is not that His course of conduct never changes to meet circumstances. But it is this—that His character never changes; that His nature and the principles that control His voluntary action remain eternally the same. All His natural—all His moral attributes remain forever unchanged. This is all that can rationally be implied in God's immutability.

Now, His hearing and answering prayer imply no change of character, no change in His principles of action. Indeed, if you ask why He ever answers prayer at all, the answer must be, because He is unchangeable.

Prayer brings the suppliant into new relations to God's kingdom; and to meet these new relations, God's unchangeable principles require him to change the course of his administration. He answers prayer because He is unchangeably benevolent. It is not because His benevolence changes, but because it does not change, that He answers prayer. Who can suppose that God's answering prayer implies any change in His moral character? For example, if a man, in prayer repents, God forgives. If he does not repent of present sin, God does not forgive. And who does not see that God's immutability must require this course at His hands?

Suppose God did not change His conduct when men change their character and their attitude toward Him. This would imply fickleness—an utter absence of fixed principles. His unchangeable goodness must therefore imply that when His creatures change morally, He changes His course and conforms to their new position. Any other view of the case is simply absurd, and only the result of ignorance. Strange that men should hold it to be inconsistent for God to change and give rain in answer to prayer, or give any needed spiritual blessings to those who ask them!

Intercourse with God is a necessity for moral beings, demanded by creatures as a necessity of their natures. No doubt this is true in heaven itself, and the fact that this want of their natures is so gloriously supplied there, makes heaven. The Bible represents spirits in heaven as praying.

We hear them crying out, "How long, O Lord, holy and true, dost thou not judge and avenge our blood on them that dwell on the earth?" (Rev. 6:10)

True, their subjects of prayer are not in all respects the same as ours; we have things to pray for which they have no occasion to ask for themselves. They are neither sick nor sinful; but can you suppose they never pray, "Thy kingdom come?" Have they lost all sympathy with those interests of Zion? Far from it. Knowing more of the value of those interests, they no doubt feel more deeply their importance, and pray more earnestly for their promotion.

From the nature of the case, God's treatment of the inhabitants of heaven must be conditioned on their voluntary course in regard to Him and His kingdom. It must be governed and determined by their knowledge, their progress in knowledge, and their improvement of the means and powers at their command. Obviously their voluntary worship, gratitude, thanksgiving, and service of every sort must vary their relations to God, and consequently, His course toward them. He will do many things to them and for them that He could not do if they did not pray, and praise, and love, and study, and labour.

This must be true even in heaven, of apostles, and prophets, and of all glorified saints. God makes to them successive revelations of Himself, each successively higher than the preceding, and all dependent on their voluntary devotion to Him and to His glory. They are forever advancing in His service, full of worship, praise, adoration, and this only prepares them the more to be sent on missions of love and service, and to be employed as the interests of God's kingdom require.

Hence, we see that God's conduct toward saints in heaven depends on their own voluntary course and bearing toward Him. This is a necessity of any and every moral system. If saints in heaven are moral agents, and God's government over them is also moral, all these results must follow. In this world sin exists; and in this fact we see an obvious necessity for this law of moral administration. But the holy in heaven are no less moral and responsible than the sinning on earth. The great object of God's administration is to assimilate moral beings to Himself; hence, He must make His treatment of them depend on their moral course toward Him.

In regard to saints on earth, how can God do them any good unless He can draw them to Himself in prayer and praise? This is one of the most evident necessities that can be named. Men irresistibly feel the propriety of confession and supplication in order to achieve forgiveness. This feeling lies among the primitive affirmations of the mind. Men know that if they would be healed of sin they must seek and find God.

II. WHY MEN SHOULD PRAY ALWAYS AND NOT FAINT

But why pray so much and so often? Why the exhortation to pray always and not to faint?

The case presented in the context is very strong. Whether it be history or supposition does not affect the merits of the case as given us to illustrate importunity in prayer. The poor widow persevered. She kept coming and would not be discouraged. By dint of perseverance simply, she succeeded. The judge who cared not for God or man, did care somewhat for his own comfort and quiet, and therefore thought it wise to listen to her story and grant her request.

Upon this case our Lord seized to enforce and encourage importunity in prayer. Hear His argument. "Shall not God," who is by no means unjust, but whose compassions are a great deep, "shall not such a God avenge His own elect, who cry day and night unto Him, though He seem to bear long" in delaying to answer their prayers? "I tell you He will avenge them speedily."

A. Men ought to pray always, because they always need the influence of prayer. Consider what is implied in prayer and what prayer does for you. Prayer bathes the soul in an atmosphere of the Divine Presence. Prayer communes with God and brings the whole mind under the hallowed influence of such communion. Prayer goes to God to seek pardon and find mercy and grace to help. How obvious, then, that we always need its influence on our hearts and lives. Truly, we need not wonder that God should enjoin it upon us to pray always.

B. God needs prayer from us as a condition of His doing to us and for us all He would. He loves us and sees a thousand blessings that we need, and that He would delight to bestow; but yet He cannot bestow them except on condition that we ask for them in Jesus' name. His treatment of us and His bestowment of blessings upon us must depend upon our views and conduct, whether we feel our dependence on Him, whether we confess and forsake all sin, whether we trust Him and thoroughly honour Him in all things. His action toward us must depend upon our attitude toward Him. It is essential in the management of a moral system that we should pray and trust, in order that He may freely and abundantly give, and especially that He may give in a way safe to us and honourable to Himself.

Nothing can be substituted for our own praying, either in its relations to God or to ourselves. We cannot get along without the personal benefit of prayer, confession, trust, and praise. You cannot substitute instruction, ever so much or so good; for these things must enter into the soul's experience; you must feel them before God, and carry out the life and power of these truths in your very heart before the Lord; else they are worse than unknown to you. You are not likely to understand many of these things without prayer; and even if you were to understand them, and yet not pray, the knowledge would only be a curse to you.

What can be so useful to us sinners as direct communion with God—the searching of the heart that it induces—the humility, the confessions, and the supplications? Other things have their use. Instruction is good; reading God's Word may be a blessing; communion with the saints is pleasant. But what are they all compared with personal intercourse with God? Nothing else can make the soul so sick of sin and so dead to the world. Nothing else breathes such spiritual life into the soul as real prayer.

Prayer also prepares us the better to receive all blessings from God, and hence should be constant.

Prayer pleases God as Governor of the Universe, because it puts us in a position in which He can bless us and gratify His own benevolence.

Search the history of the world, and you will find that where there has been most true prayer, and the soul has been most deeply imbued with the Divine Presence, there God has most abundantly and richly blessed the soul. Who does not know that holy men of old were eminent for usefulness and power according as they were faithful and mighty in prayer?

The more we pray, the more shall we be enlightened, for surely they are most enlightened who pray most. If we go no further in divine things than human reason can carry us, we get little indeed from God.

The more men pray, the more they will love prayer, and the more will they enjoy God. On the other hand, the more we pray— in real prayer—the more will God delight in us.

Observe this, which I say: Delight; the more will God truly DELIGHT in us.

This is not merely the love of benevolence, for God is benevolent to all; but He delights in His praying children in the sense of having complacency in their character. The Bible often speaks of the great interest that God takes in those who live near Him in much prayer. This is naturally and necessarily the case. Why should not God delight in those who delight in Him?

The more we pray, the more God loves to manifest to others that He delights in us, and hears our prayers. If His children live lives of much prayer, God delights to honour them, as an encouragement to others to pray. They come into a position in which He can bless them and can make His blessings on them result in good to others—thus doubly gratifying the benevolence of His heart.

WE SHALL ALWAYS NEED PRAYER.

We can never reach a position in which we shall not need prayer. Who believes that saints in heaven will have no need of prayer? True, they will have perfect faith, but this, so far from precluding prayer, only the more ensures it. Men have strangely assumed that if there were only perfect faith, prayer would cease. Nothing can be more false and groundless. Certainly, then, we never can get beyond prayer.

If I had time I should like to show how the manner of prayer varies as Christians advance in holiness. They pray not less, but more and they know better how to pray. When the natural life is mingled largely with the spiritual, there is an outward effervescing, which passes away as the soul comes nearer to God. You would suppose there is less excitement, and there is less of animal excitement; but the deep fountains of the soul flow in unbroken sympathy with God.

We can never get beyond the point where prayer is greatly useful to us. The more the heart breathes after God, and rises toward Him in heavenly aspirations, the more useful do such exercises become. The aged Christian finds Himself more and more benefited in prayer as He draws more and more near to God. The more He prays, the more He sees the wisdom and necessity of prayer for His own spiritual good.

The very fact that prayer is so great a privilege to sinners makes it most honourable to God to hear prayer. Some think it disgraceful to God. What a sentiment! It assumes that God's real greatness consists in His being so high above us as to have no regard for us whatever. Not so with God. He who regards alike the flight of an archangel and the fall of a sparrow, before whose eye no possible event is too minute for His attention—no insect too small for His notice and His love—His infinite glory is manifest in this very fact that nothing is too lofty or too low for His regard. None is too insignificant to miss sympathy—none too mean to share His kindness.

Many talk of prayer as only a duty, not a privilege; but with this view of it they cannot pray acceptably. When your children, full of wants, come running to you in prayer, do they come because it is a duty? No, indeed! They come because it is their privilege. They regard it as their privilege. Other children do not feel so toward you. And it is a wonderful privilege! Who does not know it and feel it to be so? Shall we then ever fail to avail ourselves of it?

Finally, we are sure to prevail if we thoroughly persevere and pray always, and do not faint. Let this suffice to induce perseverance in prayer. Do you need blessings? And yet are they delayed? Pray always and never faint; so shall you obtain all you need.

III. WHY MEN DO NOT PRAY ALWAYS

Many reasons exist. In the case of some, because the enmity

of their hearts toward God is such that they are shy and dread prayer. They have so strong a dislike to God, they cannot make up their minds to come near to Him in prayer.

Some are self-righteous and self-ignorant, and therefore have no heart to pray. Their self-righteousness makes them feel strong enough without prayer, and self-ignorance prevents their feeling their own real wants.

Unbelief keeps others from constant prayer. They have not confidence enough in God as ready to answer prayer. Of course, with such unbelief in their hearts, they will not pray always.

Sophistry prevents others. I have alluded to some of its forms. They say, God being immutable, never changes His course; or they urge that there is no need of prayer, inasmuch as God will surely do just right, although nobody should pray. These are little sophistries, such as ignorant minds get up and stumble over. It is amazing that any minds can be so ignorant and so unthinking as to be influenced by these sophistries. I can recollect how these objections to prayer came up many years since before my mind, but were instantly answered and set aside, they seemed so absurd. This, for instance: that God had framed the universe so wisely that there is no need of prayer, and indeed no room for it. My answer was ready. What was God's object in making and arranging His universe? Was it to show Himself to be a good mechanic, so skilful that He can make a universe to run itself, without His constant agency? Was this His object? No! But His object was to plant in this universe intelligent minds and then reveal Himself to them and draw them to love and trust their own infinite Father. This object is every way noble and worthy of a God. But the other notion is horrible! It takes from God every endearing attribute and leaves Him only a good mechanic!

The idea that God mingles His agency continually in human affairs, prevails everywhere among all minds in all ages. Everywhere they have seen God revealing Himself. They expect such revelations of God. They have believed in them, and have seen how essential this fact is to that confidence and love which belong to a moral government. It seems passing strange that men can sophisticate themselves into such nonsense as this! Insufferable nonsense are all such objections!

On one occasion, when it had been very wet and came off suddenly very dry, the question arose: *How can you vindicate the providence of God?*

At first the question stung me. I stopped, considered it a few moments, and then asked, "What can His object be in giving us weather at all? Why does He send or not send rain? If the object were to raise as many potatoes as possible, this is not the wisest course. But if the object were to make us feel our dependence, this is the wisest course possible. What if God were to raise harvests enough in one year to supply us for the next ten? We might all become atheists. We should be very likely to think we could live without God. But now every day and every year He shuts us up to depend on Himself. Who does not see that a moral government, ordered on any other system, would work ruin?"

Another reason is that men have no real sense of sin or of any spiritual want, and no consciousness of guilt. While in this state of mind, it need not be expected that men will pray.

In the other extreme, after becoming deeply convicted, they fall into despair and think it does no good to pray.

Another reason for not praying much is found in self-righteous conceptions of what is requisite to success in prayer. One says, *I am too degraded and am not good enough to pray.* This objection is founded altogether in self-righteous notions—assuming that your own goodness must be the ground or reason for God's hearing your prayer.

A reason with many for little prayer is their worldly-mindedness. Their minds are so filled with thoughts of a worldly nature, they cannot get into the spirit of prayer.

Again, in the case of some, their own experience discourages them. They have often prayed, yet with little success. This brings them into a skeptical attitude in regard to prayer. Very likely the real reason of their failure has been the lack of perseverance. They have not obeyed this precept that urges that men pray always, and never faint.

REMARKS

It is no loss of time to pray. Many think it chiefly or wholly lost time. They are so full of business, they say, and assume that prayer will spoil their business. I tell you, that your business, if it were of such sort as ought to be done at all, will go all the better for much prayer. Rise from your bed a little earlier and pray. Get time somehow—by almost any imaginable sacrifice, sooner than forego prayer.

Are you studying? It is no loss of time to pray, as I know very well by my own experience. If I am to preach with only two hours for preparation, I give one hour to prayer. If I were to study anything—let it be Virgil or Geometry, I would by all means pray first. Prayer enlarges and illumines the mind. It is like coming into the presence of a master spirit. You know how sometimes this electrifies the mind, and fires it with boundless enthusiasm. So, and much the more, does real access to God.

Let a physician pray a great deal; He needs counsel from God. Let the mechanic and the merchant pray much; they will testify, after trial of it, that God gives them counsel, and that, consequently, they lose nothing and gain much by constant prayer.

None but an eminently praying man is a safe religious teacher. However scientific and literary, if He were not a praying man, He cannot be trusted.

A spirit of prayer is of much greater value than human learning without it. If I were to choose, I would prefer intercourse with God in prayer before the intellect of Gabriel. I do not say this to disparage the value of learning and knowledge, for when great talents and learning are sanctified with much prayer, the result is a mind of mighty power.

Those who do not pray cannot understand the facts in regard to answers to prayer. How can they know? Those things seem to them utterly incredible. They have had no such experience. In fact all their experience goes in the opposite direction. State a case to them; they look incredulous. Perhaps they will say, "You seem to think you can prophesy and foreknow events!" Let them be answered, "The secret of the Lord is with them that fear him."

Those who keep up a living intercourse with God know many things they do not tell, and had better not tell.

When I was a young convert, I knew an aged lady whose piety and prayer seemed to me quite extraordinary. You could not feel like talking much in her presence; there was something in it that struck you as remarkable. The subject of sanctification came into discussion, and meeting me on one occasion, she said, "Charles, take care what you do! Don't do things to be sorry for afterwards." A son of hers became a Christian and was astonished at the manifestations of his mother's piety. She had prayed for him long and most earnestly. When, at length, his eyes were opened, she began to say, "I did not tell anybody my experiences, but in fact I have known nothing about condemnation for thirty years past. In all this time I am not aware that I have committed a known sin.

My soul has enjoyed uninterrupted communion with God, and constant access to His mercy-seat in prayer."

Prayer is the great secret of ministerial success.

Some think this secret lies in talent or in tact, but it is not so. A man may know all human knowledge, yet, without prayer, what can he do? He cannot move and control men's hearts. He can do nothing to purpose unless he lives in sympathy and open-faced communion with God. Only so can he be mighty through God to win souls to Christ. Here let me not be understood to depreciate learning and the knowledge of God. By no means. But prayer and its power are much greater and more effective. Herein lies the great mistake of Theological Seminaries and of gospel ministers. They lay excessive stress on learning, and genius, and talents. They fail to appreciate duly the paramount importance of much prayer. How much better for them to lay the principal stress on bathing the soul in God's presence! Let them rely first of all on God, who worketh mightily in His praying servants through His Spirit given them; and mediately, let them estimate above all other means, prayer—prayer that is abundant, devout, earnest, and full of living faith. Such a course would be an effectual correction of one of the most prevalent and perilous mistakes of the age.

9

PREVAILING PRAYER

"The effectual fervent prayer of a righteous man availeth much"

—James 5:16

There are two kinds of means requisite to promote a revival: the one to influence man, the other to influence God.

The truth is employed to influence men, and prayer to move God. When I speak of moving God, I do not mean that prayer changes God's mind, or that His disposition or character is changed. But prayer produces such a change in us as renders it consistent for God to do, as it would not be consistent for Him to do otherwise. When a sinner repents, that state of feeling makes it proper for God to forgive him. God has always been ready to forgive him on that condition, so that when the sinner changes his feelings and repents, it requires no change of feeling in God to pardon him. It is the sinner's repentance that renders His forgiveness proper, and is the occasion of God's acting as He does. So when Christians offer effectual prayer, their state of feeling renders it proper for God to answer them. He was never unwilling to bestow the blessing—on the condition that they felt aright, and offered the right kind of prayer.

Prayer is an essential link in the chain of causes that lead to a revival, as much so as truth is. Some have zealously used truth to convert men, and laid very little stress on prayer. They have preached, and talked, and distributed tracts with great zeal, and then wondered that they had so little success. And the reason was that they forgot to use the other branch of the means, effectual prayer. They overlooked the fact that truth, by itself, will never produce the effect, without the Spirit of God, and that the Spirit is given in answer to prayer.

Sometimes it happens that those who are the most engaged in employing truth are not the most engaged in prayer. This is always unhappy. For unless they have the spirit of prayer (or unless some one else has), the truth, by itself, will do nothing but harden men in impenitence. Probably in the Day of Judgment it will be found that nothing is ever done by the truth, used ever so zealously, unless there is a spirit of prayer somewhere in connection with the presentation of truth.

Others err in the reverse direction. Not that they lay too much stress on prayer. But they overlook the fact that prayer might be offered forever, by itself, and nothing would be done. Because sinners are not converted by direct contact of the Holy Ghost, but by the truth, employed as a means.

To expect the conversion of sinners by prayer alone, without the employment of truth, is to tempt God.

Our subject being Prevailing Prayer, I propose:

I. To show what is effectual or prevailing prayer.

II. To state some of the most essential attributes of prevailing prayer.

III. To give some reasons why God requires this kind of prayer.

IV. To show that such prayer will avail much.

I. WHAT PREVAILING PRAYER IS

A. Effectual, prevailing prayer, does not consist in benevolent desires alone.

Benevolent desires are doubtless pleasing to God. Such desires pervade heaven and are found in all holy beings. But they are not prayer. Men may have these desires as the angels and glorified spirits have them. But this is not the effectual, prevailing prayer spoken of in the text. Prevailing prayer is something more than this.

B. Prevailing, or effectual prayer, is that prayer which attains the blessing that it seeks. It is that prayer which effectually moves God. The very idea of effectual prayer is that it effects its object.

II. ESSENTIAL ATTRIBUTES OF PREVAILING PRAYER

I cannot detail in full all the things that go to make up prevailing prayer. But I will mention some things that are essential to it; some things that a person must do in order to prevail in prayer.

A. He must pray for a definite object. He need not expect to offer such prayer if he prays at random, without any distinct or definite object. He must have an object distinctly before his mind. I speak now of secret prayer. Many people go away into their rooms alone "to pray," simply because "they must say their prayers." The time has come when they are in the habit of going by themselves for prayer—in the morning, or at noon, or at whatever time of day it may be. But instead of having anything to say, any definite object before their mind, they fall down on their knees and pray for just what comes into their minds—for everything that floats in the imagination at the time, and when they have done they can hardly tell a word of what they have been praying for.

This is not effectual prayer. What should we think of anybody who should try to move a Legislature so, and should say: "Now it is winter, and the Legislature is in session, and it is time to send up petitions," and should go up to the Legislature and petition at random, without any definite object? Do you think such petitions would move the Legislature?

A man must have some definite object before his mind. He cannot pray effectually for a variety of objects at once. The mind is so constituted that it cannot fasten its desires intensely upon many things at the same time.

All the instances of effectual prayer recorded in the Bible are of this kind.

Wherever you see that the blessing sought for in prayer was attained, you will find that the prayer that was offered was prayer for that definite object.

B. Prayer, to be effectual, must be in accordance with the revealed will of God. To pray for things contrary to the revealed will of God is to tempt God. There are three ways in which God's will is revealed to men for their guidance in prayer.

1. By express promises or predictions in the Bible, that He will give or do certain things; promises in regard to particular things, or in general terms, so that we may apply them to particular things. For instance, there is this promise: "What things soever ye desire when ye pray, believe that ye receive them, and ye shall have them" (Mark 11:24).

2. By His Providence. When He makes it clear that such and such events are about to take place, it is as much a revelation as if He had written it in His Word. It would be impossible to reveal everything in the Bible. But God often makes it clear to those who have spiritual discernment that it is His will to grant such and such blessings.

3. By His Spirit. When God's people are at a loss what to pray for, agreeable to His will, His Spirit often instructs them. Where there is no particular revelation, and Providence leaves it dark, and we know not what to pray for as we ought, we are expressly told that "the Spirit also helpeth our infirmities," and "the Spirit itself maketh intercession for us with groanings which cannot be uttered" (Romans 8:26). A great deal has been said on the subject of praying in faith for things not revealed. It is objected that this doctrine implies a new revelation. I answer that, new or old, it is the very revelation that Jehovah says He makes. It is just as plain here as if it were now revealed by a voice from heaven, that the Spirit of God helps the people of God to pray according to the will of God, when they themselves know not what they ought to pray for. "And He that searcheth the hearts knoweth what is the mind of the Spirit, because He maketh intercession for the saints according to the will of God" (Romans 8:27); and He leads Christians to pray for just those things, "with groanings which cannot be uttered." When neither the Word nor Providence enables them to decide, let them be "filled with the Spirit," as God commands them: "Be filled with the Spirit" (Ephesians 5:18). And He will lead their minds to such things as God is willing to grant.

To pray effectually you must pray with submission to the will of God. Do not confound submission with indifference. No two things are more unlike. I once knew an individual who came where there was a revival. He himself was cold, and did not enter into the spirit of it, and had no spirit of prayer; and when he heard the brethren pray as if they could not be denied, he was shocked at their boldness, and kept all the time insisting on the importance of praying with submission; when it was as plain as anything could be that he confounded submission with indifference.

Again, do not confound submission in prayer with a general confidence that God will do what is right. It is proper to have this confidence that God will do right in all things. But this is a different thing from submission. What I mean by submission in prayer is acquiescence in the revealed will of God. To submit to any command of God is to obey it.

Submission to some supposable or possible, but secret, decree of God is not submission. To submit to any dispensation of Providence is impossible till it comes. For we never can know what the event is to be, till it takes place.

Take a case: David, when his child was sick, was distressed, and agonized in prayer, and refused to be comforted. He took it so much to heart that when the child died his servants were afraid to tell him. But as soon as he heard that the child was dead, he laid aside his grief, and arose, and asked for food, and ate and drank as usual. While the child was yet alive he did not know what was the will of God, and so he fasted and prayed, and, "Who can tell whether God will be gracious to me, that my child may live?" He did not know but that his prayer, his agony, was the very thing on which it turned, whether the child was to live or not. He thought that if he humbled himself and entreated God, perhaps God would spare him this blow. But as soon as God's will was clear, and the child was dead, he bowed like a saint. He seemed not only to acquiesce, but also actually to take a satisfaction in it. "I shall go to him, but he shall not return to me" (2 Samuel 12:15-23). This was true submission. He reasoned correctly in the case. While he had no revelation of the will of God he did not know but that the child's recovery depended on his prayer. But when he had a revelation of the will of God, he submitted. While the will of God is not known, to submit without prayer is tempting God. Perhaps, and for all you know, the fact of your offering the right kind of prayer may be the thing on which the event turns. In the case of an impenitent friend, the very condition on which he is to be saved from hell may be the fervency and importunity of your prayer for that individual.

D. Effectual prayer for an object implies a desire for that object commensurate with its importance. If a person truly desires any blessing, his desires will bear some proportion to the greatness of the blessing. The desires of the Lord Jesus Christ for the blessing He prayed for were amazingly strong, amounting even to agony. If the desire for an object is strong, and is a benevolent desire, and the thing is not contrary to the will and providence of God, the presumption is that it will be granted. There are two reasons for this presumption:

1. From the general benevolence of God. If it is a desirable object; if, so far as we can see, it would be an act of benevolence in God to grant it, His general benevolence is presumptive evidence that He will grant it.

2. If you find yourself exercised with benevolent desires for any object, there is a strong presumption that the Spirit of God is exciting these very desires, and stirring you up to pray for that object, so that it may be granted in answer to prayer. In such a case no degree of desire or importunity in prayer is improper. A Christian may come up, as it were, and take hold of the hand of God. See the case of Jacob, when he exclaimed, in an agony of desire: "I will not let Thee go except Thou bless me" (Genesis

32:26). Was God displeased with his boldness and importunity? Not at all; but He granted him the very thing he prayed for. So in the case of Moses. God said to him: "Let Me alone, that My wrath may wax hot against them, and that I may consume them; and I will make of thee a great nation" (Exodus 32:10). What did Moses do? Did he stand aside and let God do as He said? No, his mind ran back to the Egyptians, and he thought how they would triumph. "Wherefore should the Egyptians say, For mischief did He bring them out?" It seemed as if he took hold of the uplifted hand of God, to avert the blow. Did God rebuke him and tell him he had no business to interfere? No. It seemed as if He was unable to deny anything to such importunity, and so Moses stood in the gap, and prevailed upon God. Prevailing prayer is often offered in the present day, when Christians have been wrought up to such a pitch of importunity and such a holy boldness that afterwards when they looked back upon it, they were frightened and amazed at themselves, to think they should have dared to exercise such importunity with God. And yet these prayers have prevailed, and obtained the blessing. And many of these persons, with whom I am acquainted, are among the holiest persons I know in the world.

E. Prayer, to be effectual, must be offered from right motives. Prayer should not be selfish, but should be dictated by a supreme regard for the glory of God. A great deal is offered from pure selfishness.

Women sometimes pray for their husbands, that they may be converted, because, they say, "It would be so much more pleasant to have my husband go to Church with me," and all that. And they seem never to lift up their thoughts above self at all. They do not seem to think how their husbands are dishonouring God by their sins, or how God would be glorified in their conversion.

So it is very often with parents. They cannot bear to think that their children should be lost. They pray for them very earnestly indeed. But if you talk with them upon the subject, they are very tender about it and tell you how good their children are: how they respect religion, and how they are, indeed, "almost Christians now." They talk as if they were afraid you would hurt their children by simply telling them the truth. They do not think how such amiable and lovely children are dishonouring God by their sins; they are only thinking what a dreadful thing it will be for them to go to hell. Unless their thoughts rise higher than this, their prayers will never prevail with a holy God. The temptation to selfish motives is so strong that there is reason to fear a great many parental prayers never rise above the yearnings of parental tenderness. And that is the reason why so many prayers are not answered and why so many pious, praying parents have ungodly children.

Much of the prayer for the heathen world seems to be based on no higher principle than sympathy. Missionary agents and others are dwelling almost exclusively upon the six hundred millions of heathens going to hell, while little is said of their dishonouring God. This is a great evil, and until the Church learns to have higher motives for prayer and missionary effort than sympathy for the heathen, her prayers and efforts will never amount to much.

F. Prayer, to be effectual, must be by the intercession of the Spirit. You never can expect to offer prayer according to the will of God without the Spirit. In the first two cases, it is not because Christians are unable to offer such prayer, where the will of God is revealed in His Word or indicated by His providence. They are able to do it, just as they are able to be holy. But the fact is, that they are so wicked that they never do offer such prayer, unless the Spirit of God influences them. There must be a faith, such as is produced by the effectual operation of the Holy Ghost.

G. It must be persevering prayer. As a general thing, Christians who have backslidden and lost the spirit of prayer will not get at once into the habit of persevering prayer. Their minds are not in a right state, and they cannot fix their thoughts so as to hold on till the blessing comes. If their minds were in that state in which they would persevere till the answer came, effectual prayer might be offered at once, as well as after praying ever so many times for an object. But they have to pray again and again, because their thoughts are so apt to wander away and are so easily diverted from the object.

Most Christians come up to prevailing prayer by a protracted process. Their minds gradually become filled with anxiety about an object, so that they will even go about their business sighing out their desires to God.

Consider the mother whose child is sick. She goes around her house sighing as if her heart would break. And if she is a praying mother, her sighs are breathed out to God all day long. If she goes out of the room where her child is, her mind is still on it; and if she is asleep, still her thoughts are on it, and she starts in her dreams, thinking that perhaps it may be dying. Her whole mind is absorbed in that sick child. This is the state of mind in which Christians offer prevailing prayer.

For what reason did Jacob wrestle all night in prayer with God? He knew that he had done his brother Esau a great injury in getting away the birthright, a long time before. And now he was informed that his injured brother was coming to meet him with an armed force, altogether too powerful to contend with. And there was great reason to suppose that Esau was coming with a purpose of revenge. There were two reasons then why Jacob should be distressed. The first was that he had done this great injury and had never made any reparation. The other was that Esau was coming with a force sufficient to crush him. Now what did he do? He first arranged everything in the best manner he could to placate and meet his brother: sending his present first, then his property, then his family, putting those he loved most farthest behind. And by that time his mind was so exercised that he could not contain himself. He went away alone over the brook and poured out his very soul in an agony of prayer all night.

And just as the day was breaking, the Angel of the Covenant said, "Let me go." Jacob's whole being was, as it were, agonized at the thought of giving up, and he cried out, "I will not let Thee go, except Thou bless me."

His soul was wrought up into an agony, and he obtained the blessing, but he always bore the marks of it, and showed that his body had been greatly affected by this mental struggle. This is prevailing prayer.

Now, do not deceive yourselves with thinking that you offer effectual prayer, unless you have this intense desire for the blessing. I do not believe in it. Prayer is not effectual unless it is offered up with an agony of desire.

The apostle Paul speaks of it as travail of the soul. Jesus Christ, when He was praying in the garden, was in such an agony that "His sweat was as it were great drops of blood falling down to the ground" (Luke 22:44). I have never known a person sweat blood; but I have known a person pray till the blood ran from his nose. And I have known persons pray till they were all wet with perspiration, in the coldest weather in winter. I have known persons pray for hours, till their strength was all exhausted with the agony of their minds. Such prayers prevailed with God.

This agony in prayer was prevalent in President Edwards' day, in the revivals that then took place. It was one of the great stumbling blocks in those days to persons who were opposed to the revival, that people used to pray till their body was overpowered with their feelings. I will give a paragraph of what President

Edwards says on the subject, to let you see that this is not a new thing in the Church, but has always prevailed wherever revivals prevailed with power. It is from his *Thoughts on Revivals*:

"We cannot determine that God shall never give any person so much of a discovery of Himself, not only as to weaken their bodies, but to take away their lives. It is supposed by very learned and judicious divines, that Moses' life was taken away after this manner, and this has also been supposed to be the case with some other saints.

"If God gives a great increase of discoveries of Himself and of love to Him, the benefit is infinitely greater than the calamity, though the life should presently after be taken away . . .

"There is one particular kind of exercise and concern of mind that many have been empowered by, that has been especially stumbling to some; and that is, the deep concern and distress that they have been in for the souls of others. I am sorry that any put us to the trouble of doing that which seems so needless, as defending such a thing as this. It seems like mere trifling in so plain a case, to enter into a formal and particular debate, in order to determine whether there be anything in the greatness and importance of the case that will answer and bear a proportion to the greatness of the concern that some have manifested. Men may be allowed, from no higher a principle than common ingenuousness and humanity, to be very deeply concerned, and greatly exercised in mind, at seeing others in great danger of no greater a calamity than drowning or being burned up in a house on fire. And if so, then doubtless it will be allowed to be equally reasonable, if they saw them in danger of a calamity ten times greater, to be still much more concerned: and so much more still, if the calamity were still vastly greater. And why, then, should it be thought unreasonable and looked upon with a very suspicious eye, as if it must come from some bad cause, when persons are extremely concerned at seeing others in very great danger of suffering the wrath of Almighty God to all eternity? And besides, it will doubtless be allowed that those that have very great degrees of the Spirit of God, that is, a spirit of love, may well be supposed to have vastly more of love and compassion to their fellow creatures than those that are influenced only by common humanity.

"Why should it be thought strange that those that are full of the Spirit of Christ should be proportionally in their love to souls, like Christ?—who had so strong a love for them, and concern for them, as to be willing to drink the dregs of the cup of God's fury for them; and at the same time that He offered up His blood for souls, offered up also, as their High Priest, strong crying and tears, with an extreme agony, wherein the soul of Christ was, as it were, in travail for the souls of the elect; and, therefore in saving them He is said to 'see of the travail of His soul.' As such a spirit of love to, and concern for, souls was the spirit of Christ, so it is the spirit of the Church; and therefore the Church, in desiring and seeking that Christ might be brought forth in the world, and in the souls of men, is represented (Revelation 12:1, 2) as 'a woman crying, travailing in birth, and pained to be delivered.'

"The spirit of those that have been in distress for the souls of others, so far as I can discern, seems not to be different from that of the apostle, who travailed for souls, and was ready to wish himself accursed from Christ for others (Romans 9:3). Nor from that of the Psalmist (Psalm 119:53): 'Horror hath taken hold upon me, because of the wicked that forsake Thy law.' And (ver. 136): 'Rivers of waters run down mine eyes, because they keep not Thy law.' Nor from that of the prophet Jeremiah (4:19): 'My bowels, my bowels! I am pained at my very heart; my heart maketh a noise in me: I cannot hold my peace, because Thou hast heard, O my soul, the sound of the trumpet, the alarm of war.' And so chapter 9:1, and 13:17, and Isaiah 22:4. We read of Mordecai, when he saw his people in danger of being destroyed with a temporal destruction

(Esther 4:1) that he 'rent his clothes, and put on sackcloth with ashes, and went out into the midst of the city, and cried with a loud and a bitter cry.' And why then should persons be thought to be distracted when they cannot forbear crying out at the consideration of the misery of those that are going to eternal destruction?"

I have quoted this to show that this thing was common in the great revivals of those days. It has always been so in all great revivals, and has been more or less common in proportion to the greatness, and extent, and depth of the work. It was so in the great revivals in Scotland, and multitudes used to be overpowered, and some almost died by the depth of their agony.

So also, prayer prevailed at Cambuslang (1741-1742) in the revival under William McCulloch and Whitefield. When Whitefield reached Cambuslang he immediately preached on the braeside to a vast congregation (on a Tuesday at noon). At six o'clock he preached again, and a third time at nine. Then McCulloch took up the parable and preached till one in the morning. And still the people were unwilling to leave. So many were convicted, crying to God for mercy, that Whitefield described the scene as "a very field of battle." On the ensuing Communion Sunday, Whitefield preached to twenty thousand people; and again on the Monday, when he said, "You might have seen thousands bathed in tears, some at the same time wringing their hands, others almost swooning, and others crying out and mourning over a pierced Saviour. It was like the Passover in Josiah's time." On the voyage from London to Scotland, prior to this campaign, Whitefield had "spent most of his time on board ship in secret prayer." (See Gledstone's "George Whitefield, M.A., Field Preacher.")

H. If you mean to pray effectually, you must pray a great deal. It was said of the Apostle James that after he was dead it was found that his knees were callused like a camel's knees, from praying so much. Ah, here was the secret of the success of those primitive ministers! They had callused knees!

I. If you intend prayer to be effectual, you must offer it in the name of Christ. You cannot come to God in your own name. You cannot plead your own merits. But you can come in a name that is always acceptable.

You all know what it is to use the name of a man. If you should go to the bank with a draft or note endorsed by John Jacob Astor, that would be giving you his name, and you know you could get the money from the bank just as well as he could himself. Now, Jesus Christ gives you the use of His name. And when you pray in the name of Christ the meaning of it is, that you can prevail just as well as He could Himself, and receive just as much as God's well beloved Son would if He were to pray Himself for the same things. But you must pray in faith.

J. You cannot prevail in prayer without renouncing all your sins. You must not only recall them to mind, and repent of them, but you must actually renounce them, and leave them off, and in the purpose of your heart renounce them all for ever.

K. You must pray in faith. You must expect to obtain the things for which you ask. You need not look for an answer to prayer, if you pray without any expectation of obtaining it. You are not to form such expectations without any reason for them. In the cases I have supposed, there is a reason for the expectation. In case the thing is revealed in God's Word, if you pray without an expectation of receiving the blessings, you just make God a liar. If the will of God is indicated by His providence, you ought to depend on it, according to the clearness of the indication, so far as to expect the blessing if you pray for it. And if you are led by His Spirit to pray for certain things, you have as much reason to expect those things to be done as if God had revealed it in His Word.

But some say, "Will not this view of the leadings of the Spirit of God lead people into fanaticism?" I answer that I know not but many may deceive themselves in respect to this matter. Multitudes have deceived themselves in regard to all the other points of religion. And if some people should think the Spirit of God leads them, when it is nothing but their own imagination, is that any reason why those who know that the Spirit leads them should not follow the Spirit?

Many people suppose themselves to be converted when they are not. Is that any reason why we should not cleave to the Lord Jesus Christ?

Suppose some people are deceived in thinking they love God. Is that any reason why the pious saint who knows he has the love of God shed abroad in his heart should not give vent to his feelings in songs of praise?

Some may deceive themselves in thinking the Spirit of God leads them. But there is no need of being deceived. If people follow impulses, it is their own fault. I do not want you to follow impulses. I want you to be sober minded, and follow the sober, rational leadings of the Spirit of God. There are those who understand what I mean, and who know very well what it is to give themselves up to the Spirit of God in prayer.

III. WHY GOD REQUIRES SUCH PRAYER

I will state some of the reasons why these things are essential to effectual prayer. Why does God require such prayer, such strong desires, and such agonizing supplications?

A. These strong desires strongly illustrate the strength of God's feelings.

They are like the real feelings of God for impenitent sinners. When I have seen, as I sometimes have, the amazing strength of love for souls that has been felt by Christians, I have been wonderfully impressed with the amazing love of God, and His desires for their salvation. The case of a certain woman, of whom I read, in a revival, made the greatest impression on my mind. She had such an unutterable compassion and love for souls that she actually panted for breath. What must be the strength of the desire which God feels, when His Spirit produces in Christians such amazing agony, such throes of soul, such travail—God has chosen the best word to express it: it is travail—travail of the soul.

I have seen a man of as much strength of intellect and muscle as any man in the community fall down prostrate, absolutely overpowered by his unutterable desires for sinners. I know this is a stumbling block to many; and it always will be as long as there remain in the Church so many blind and stupid professors of religion. But I cannot doubt that these things are the work of the Spirit of God. Oh, that the whole Church could be so filled with the Spirit as to travail in prayer, till a nation should be born in a day!

It is said in the Word of God "as soon as Zion travailed, she brought forth" (Isaiah 66:8). What does that mean? I asked a professor of religion this question once. He was taking exception to our ideas of effectual prayer, and I asked what he supposed was meant by Zion's travailing.

"Oh," said he, "It means that as soon as the Church shall walk together in the fellowship of the Gospel, then it will be said that Zion travels! This walking together is called traveling." Not the same term, you see.

B. These strong desires that I have described are the natural results of great benevolence and clear views regarding the

danger of sinners. It is perfectly reasonable that it should be so. If the women who are present should look up yonder and see a family burning to death in a fire and hear their shrieks, and behold their agony, they would feel distressed, and it is very likely that many of them would faint away with agony. And nobody would wonder at it, or say they were fools or crazy to feel so much distressed at such an awful sight. It would be thought strange if there were not some expressions of powerful feeling. Why is it any wonder, then, if Christians should feel as I have described when they have clear views of the state of sinners, and the awful danger they are in? The fact is that those individuals who never have felt so, have never felt much real benevolence. Their piety must be of a very superficial character. I do not mean to judge harshly, or to speak unkindly, but I state it as a simple matter of fact; and people may talk about it as they please, but I know such piety is superficial. This is not censoriousness, but plain truth.

People sometimes "wonder at Christians having such feelings." Wonder at what? Why, at the natural, and philosophical, and necessary results of deep piety toward God, and deep benevolence toward man, in view of the great danger they see sinners to be in.

C. The soul of a Christian, when it is thus burdened, must have relief. God rolls this weight upon the soul of a Christian, for the purpose of bringing him nearer to Himself. Christians are often so unbelieving that they will not exercise proper faith in God till He rolls this burden upon them so heavily that they cannot live under it, but must go to Him for relief. It is like the case of many a convicted sinner. God is willing to receive him at once, if he will come right to Him, with faith in Jesus Christ. But the sinner will not come. He hangs back, and struggles, and groans under the burden of his sins, and will not throw himself upon God, till his burden of conviction becomes so great that he can live no longer; and when he is driven to desperation, as it were, and feels as if he were ready to sink into hell, he makes a mighty plunge, and throws himself upon God's mercy as his only hope. It was his duty to come before. God had no delight in his distress, for its own sake.

So, when professors of religion get loaded down with the weight of souls, they often pray again and again, and yet the burden is not gone, nor their distress abated, because they have never thrown it all upon God in faith.

But they cannot get rid of the burden. So long as their benevolence continues, it will remain and increase; and unless they resist and quench the Holy Ghost, they can get no relief, until, at length, when they are driven to extremity, they make a desperate effort, roll the burden upon the Lord Jesus Christ, and exercise a childlike confidence in Him. Then they feel relieved; then they feel as if the soul they were praying for would be saved. The burden is gone, and God seems in kindness to soothe the mind with a sweet assurance that the blessing will be granted. Often, after a Christian has had this struggle, this agony in prayer, and has obtained relief in this way, you will find the sweetest and most heavenly affections flow out—the soul rests sweetly and gloriously in God, and rejoices "with joy unspeakable and full of glory"

Do any of you think that there are no such things now in the experience of believers?

If I had time, I could show you, from President Edwards and other approved writers, cases and descriptions just like this. Do you ask why we never have such things here? I tell you it is not at all because you are so much wiser than Christians are in rural districts, or because you have so much more intelligence or more enlarged views of the nature of religion, or a more stable and well regulated piety. I tell you, no; instead of priding yourselves in being free from such extravagances, you ought to hide your heads, because Christians in the city are so worldly, and have so much starch, and pride, and fashion, that they cannot come down to such spirituality as this. I wish it could be so. Oh, that there might be such a spirit in this city and in this Church! I know it would make a noise if we had such things done here. But I would not care for that. Let them say, if they please, that the folks in Chatham Chapel are getting deranged. We need not be afraid of that, if we live near enough to God to enjoy His Spirit in the manner I have described.

D. These effects of the spirit of prayer upon the body are themselves no part of religion. It is only that the body is often so weak that the feelings of the soul overpower it. These bodily effects are not at all essential to prevailing prayer; but are only a natural or physical result of highly excited emotions of the mind. It is not at all unusual for the body to be weakened, and even overcome, by any powerful emotion of the mind, on other subjects besides religion. In the time of the Revolution, the doorkeeper of Congress fell down dead after receiving some highly cheering intelligence. I knew a woman in Rochester who was in a great agony of prayer for the conversion of her son-in-law. One morning he was at an anxious meeting, and she remained at home praying for him. At the close of the meeting he came home a convert, and she was so rejoiced that she fell down and died on the spot. It is no more strange that these effects should be produced by religion than by strong feeling on any other subject.

It is not essential to prayer, but is the natural result of great efforts of the mind.

E. Doubtless one great reason why God requires the exercise of this agonizing prayer is that it forms such a bond of union between Christ and the Church. It creates such sympathy between them. It is as if Christ came and poured the overflowing of His own benevolent heart into His people, and led them to sympathize and to cooperate with Him, as they never do in any other way. They feel just as Christ feels—so full of compassion for sinners that they cannot contain themselves. Thus it is often with those ministers who are distinguished for their success in preaching to sinners; they often have such compassion, such overflowing desires for their salvation, that these are shown in their speaking, and their preaching, just as though Jesus Christ spoke through them. The words come from their lips fresh and warm, as if from the very heart of Christ. I do not mean that He dictates their words; but He excites the feelings that give utterance to them. Then you see a movement in the hearers, as if Christ Himself spoke through lips of clay.

F. This travailing in birth for souls creates also a remarkable bond of union between warm-hearted Christians and the young converts. Those who are converted appear very dear to the hearts that have had this spirit of prayer for them. The feeling is like that of a mother for her first-born. Paul expresses it beautifully when he says: "My little children!" His heart was warm and tender to them. "My little children, of whom I travail in birth again"—they had backslidden, and he has all the agonies of a parent over a wandering child—"I travail in birth again until Christ be formed in you" (Galatians 4:19); "Christ, the hope of glory" (Colossians 1:27). In a revival, I have often noticed how those who had the spirit of prayer, loved the young converts. I know this is all so much algebra to those who have never felt it. But to those who have experienced the agony of wrestling, prevailing prayer, for the conversion of a soul, you may depend upon it, that soul, after it is converted, appears as dear as a child is to the mother. He has agonized for it, received it in answer to prayer, and can present it before the Lord Jesus Christ, saying: "Behold, I and the children whom the Lord hath given me" (Isaiah 8:18. See also Hebrews 2:13).

G. Another reason why God requires this sort of prayer is, that it is the only way in which the Church can be properly prepared to receive great blessings without being injured by them. When the Church is thus prostrated in the dust before God, and is in the depth of agony in prayer, the blessing does them good. While at the same time, if they had received the blessing without this deep prostration of soul, it would have puffed them up with pride. But as it is, it increases their holiness, their love, and their humility.

IV. SUCH PRAYER WILL AVAIL MUCH.

The prophet Elijah mourned over the declensions of the house of Israel, and when he saw that no other means were likely to be effectual, to prevent a perpetual going away into idolatry, he prayed that the judgments of God might come upon the guilty nation. He prayed that it might not rain, and God shut up the heavens for three years and six months, till the people were driven to the last extremity. And when he sees that it is time to relent what does he do? See him go up to the mountain and bow down in prayer. He wished to be alone; and he told his servant to go seven times, while he was agonizing in prayer. The last time, the servant told him that a little cloud had appeared, like a man's hand, and he instantly arose from his knees—the blessing was obtained. The time had come for the calamity to be turned back. "Ah, but," you say, "Elijah was a prophet."

Now, do not make this objection. They made it in the apostle's days, and what does the apostle say? Why he brought forward this very instance, and the fact that Elijah was a man of like passions with ourselves, as a case of prevailing prayer, and insisted that they should pray so too (1 Kings 17:1; 18:41-5; James 5:17).

John Knox was a man famous for his power in prayer, so that Queen Mary of England used to say that she feared his prayers more than all the armies of Europe. And events showed that she had reason to do it. He used to be in such an agony for the deliverance of his country, that he could not sleep. He had a place in his garden where he used to go to pray.

One night he and several friends were praying together, and as they prayed, Knox spoke and said that deliverance had come. He could not tell what had happened, but he felt that something had taken place, for God had heard their prayers. What was it? Why, the next news they had was, that Mary was dead!

Take a fact that was related in my hearing by a minister. He said that in a certain town there had been no revival for many years; the Church was nearly extinct, the youth were all unconverted, and desolation reigned unbroken. There lived in a retired part of the town, an aged man, a blacksmith by trade, and of so stammering a tongue that it was painful to hear him speak. On one Friday, as he was at work in his shop, alone, his mind became greatly exercised about the state of the Church and of the impenitent. His agony became so great that he was induced to lay by his work, lock the shop door, and spend the afternoon in prayer.

He prevailed, and on the Sabbath called on the minister and desired him to appoint a "conference meeting." After some hesitation, the minister consented; observing however, that he feared but few would attend. He appointed it the same evening at a large private house. When evening came, more assembled than could be accommodated in the house. All were silent for a time, until one sinner broke out in tears, and said, if any one could pray, would he pray for him? Another followed, and another, and still another, until it was found that persons from every quarter of the town were under deep conviction. And what was remarkable was, that they all dated their conviction at the hour that the old man was praying in his shop. A powerful revival followed. Thus this old stammering man prevailed, and as a prince had power with God.

REMARKS

A great deal of prayer is lost, and many people never prevail in prayer, because, when they have desires for particular blessings, they do not follow them up. They may have desires, benevolent and pure, which are excited by the Spirit of God; and when they have them, they should persevere in prayer, for if they turn off their attention, they will quench the Spirit. When you find these holy desires in your minds:

1. Do not quench the Spirit.

2. Do not be diverted to other objects. Follow the leadings of the Spirit till you have offered that "effectual fervent prayer" that "availeth much" (James 5:16).

Without the spirit of prayer, ministers will do but little good. A minister need not expect much success unless he prays for it. Sometimes others may have the spirit of prayer and obtain a blessing on his labors. Generally, however, those preachers are the most successful who have most of the spirit of prayer themselves.

Not only must ministers have the spirit of prayer, but also it is necessary that the Church should unite in offering that effectual fervent prayer which can prevail with God. "I will yet for this be inquired of by the house of Israel, to do it for them" (Ezekiel 36:37).

Now I have only to ask you, in regard to what I have set forth: "Will you do it?" Have you done what I said to you at the last Lecture? Have you gone over your sins, and confessed them, and got them all out of the way?

Can you pray now? And will you join and offer prevailing prayer that the Spirit of God may come down here?

10

CONDITIONS OF PREVAILING PRAYER

PART 1

May 26, 1847
From: *The Oberlin Evangelist*

> *"Ask, and it shall be given you."*
>
> —Matthew 7:7-8

> *"Ye ask and receive not, because ye ask amiss, to consume it upon your lusts."*
>
> —James 4:3

These passages are chosen as the foundation of several discourses that I design to preach on the **Condition of Prevailing Prayer**.

PRAYER AND ANSWER TO PRAYER

Before entering directly upon the consideration of those conditions, however, I deem it important to make several remarks upon the general subject of prayer and answer to prayer. These will occupy our attention on the present occasion.

The Bible most unequivocally asserts that all that is properly called prayer is heard and answered. "Every one that asketh," that is, in the scriptural sense of the term, "receiveth, and he that seeketh, findeth." This declaration is perfectly explicit and to the point.

Prayer is not always answered according to the letter, but often only according to the spirit.

This is a very important distinction. It can be made plain by an example taken from scripture. Paul informs us that he was afflicted with a thorn in the flesh. He has not told us precisely what this was. He calls it his "temptation that was in the flesh," and implies that it was a snare and a trouble to him, and a thing which might naturally injure his influence as an apostle. For this latter reason, probably, he was led to "beseech the Lord thrice that it might depart from him." This prayer was obviously acceptable to God, and was graciously answered. However, you will observe that it was answered not in the letter of it, but only in its spirit. The letter of the prayer specified the removal of this thorn in the flesh; and in this view of his prayer it was not answered. The spirit of the prayer was doubtless that his influence might not be injured, and that his "temptation" from this evil thing, whatever it was, might not overpower him and draw him into sin. Thus far, and in these respects, his prayer was answered.

The Lord assured him, saying, "My grace is sufficient for thee;

for my strength is made perfect in weakness."

This was a real answer to Paul's prayer, although it did not follow the particular way of doing it that Paul had named in his prayer. Paul had asked that certain desired results might be secured to him in a particular manner. The results sought constituted the spirit of the prayer; the specified manner constituted the letter. The Lord secured to him the results, perhaps even more fully than Paul expected or specifically asked; but He did it not in Paul's specified way, but in His own.

So it often happens when we pray.

The ways of the Lord are so much wiser than our own, that He kindly and most benevolently declines to follow our way, and takes His own. The result we seek, if our prayer is acceptable to Him, He will certainly secure . . . perhaps more perfectly in His own way than He could in ours.

DISTINCTIONS BETWEEN THE LETTER AND THE SPIRIT OF PRAYER

If we suppose that prayer must always be answered according to the *letter*, we are greatly mistaken. But God will always answer the *spirit* of acceptable prayer. If the letter and the spirit of prayer are identical, the Lord will answer both. When they are not identical, He may answer only according to its spirit.

No person can be saved unless in such a state of mind as to offer acceptable prayer. No man can be justified before God at all, unless in such a state of mind as would be accepted in prayer. This is so plain as to need no proof—so plain as to preclude all doubt.

Many things are really answers to prayers that are not recog-

nized as such by the suppliant or observers.

Inability to recognize the answer to prayer is common in cases where the spirit and the letter of prayer are diverse from each other. An observer, of course, is not likely to notice anything but the letter of another's prayer. Consequently, if his prayer is answered only in the spirit of it, and not in the letter at all, he will fail to recognize the answer.

And the same thing may occur in respect to the suppliant himself. Unless he notices particularly the inner state of his own mind, he may not get definitely before his eye the real thing that constitutes the spirit of his own prayer. If his attention is chiefly turned toward the letter of it, he may receive an answer to its spirit, and may not notice it as a real answer to his prayer.

The acceptable prayer of any Christian may be quite a different thing from what others suppose it to be, and sometimes different from what he supposes. In such cases, the answer will often fail to be recognized as an answer. Hence it is of vital importance that we should ourselves understand the real spirit of our own prayer.

All this applies yet more frequently in respect to observers than to the suppliant himself. Observers see only the letter of a prayer and not the spirit. Hence if the latter is answered and not the former, they will naturally suppose that the prayer is not answered, when really it is answered and in the best possible way.

Skeptics often stand by tauntingly, and cry out, "You Christians are always praying; but your prayers are never answered." Yet God may be really answering their prayers in the spirit of them, and in the most effectual and glorious manner. I think I could name many instances in which, while skeptics were triumphing as if God did not hear prayer, He was really hearing it in regard to the true spirit of it, and in such a way as most signally to glorify Himself.

Much that is called prayer is not answered in any sense whatever, and is not real prayer. Much that goes under the name of prayer is offered merely for the form of it, with neither care nor expectation to be answered. Those who pray thus will not watch to see whether their prayers are answered in any sense whatever.

For example, there are some who pray as a matter of cold duty only because they must, and not because they feel the need of some specific blessing. Hence their prayers are nothing but forms. Their hearts are not set upon any particular object. They only care to do what they call a duty; they do not care with anxious heart for any object they may specify in their prayers. Hence the thing they really care for is not the thing they pray for. In words they pray for this thing, in heart for quite another thing. The evidence of this is in the fact that they never question whether or not their prayers have been answered. If they prayed in heart for anything, they would certainly look to see if the blessing asked for is given.

Suppose a man had petitioned for some appointment to office, and had sent on his application to the president or to the appointing power. Probably his heart would be greatly set on attaining it. If so, you would have seen him watching the mail for the reply to his communication. Every day you might have seen him at the office ready to seize his letter at the earliest possible moment. But if on the other hand, he had applied only for form's sake and cared nothing about the office, or had not at all expected it, you would have seen him about other business or pleasure, things that he did care for.

The latter case rarely occurs in human affairs, but in religious matters nothing is more common. Multitudes are engaged from time to time in what they call "praying," their object being only to appease their consciences, not to obtain any desired blessing. Of course, the quiet of their consciences is the only thing they really seek by prayer, so it would be absurd for them to look for any other answers than this. They are not wont to be guilty of this absurdity.

Of course those who pray thus are not disappointed if they are not heard. It is so in case of petitions addressed to men; it is so naturally when petitions are addressed to God.

GOD ANSWERS PRAYER IN WISDOM AND LOVE

A real Christian sometimes asks in the letter of prayer for what he finds God cannot give. In such a case he can be satisfied only with the consideration that God always exercises His own infinite wisdom and His no less infinite love. If the Christian is in the true spirit of prayer, the great thing that lays nearest his heart will be granted: namely, that God may be honoured in the exercise of His own wisdom and love. This God will surely do. So, therefore, the spirit of his prayer will be granted.

It deserves special notice that those who pray as a matter of form only, and with no heart set upon the blessing named in the prayer, never ask why their prayers are not answered. Their minds are entirely at ease on this point, because they feel no solicitude about the answer at all. They did not pray for the sake of an answer. Hence they will never trouble themselves to inquire.

How many of you who hear me now know why you so rarely look for any answer to your prayers, or why you care so little about it, if your mind should chance to advert to it at all?

Again, when our petitions are not answered either in *letter* or *spirit*, it is because we have not fulfilled the revealed conditions of acceptable prayer.

CONDITIONS OF ACCEPTABLE PRAYER

Many people seem to overlook the fact that there are conditions of acceptable prayer revealed in the Bible. But this is a fact by far too important to be ever overlooked. It surely becomes every Christian to know not only that there are conditions, but also what they are.

Let us, then, fully understand that if our prayers are not answered, it is because we have failed of fulfilling the revealed conditions. This must be the reason that our prayers are not answered, for God has assured us in His word that all real prayer is always answered.

Nothing can be more important than that we should thoroughly understand the conditions of prevailing prayer. If we fail thus to understand them, we shall very probably fail to fulfill them, and of course fail to offer prevailing prayer. Alas, how ruinous a failure must this be to any soul!

There are those, I am aware, who do not expect to influence God by their prayers; they expect to produce effects upon themselves only. They hope by means of prayer to bring themselves to a better state of mind, and this is all they expect to gain by means of prayer.

WHEN ALL YOU EXPECT OF PRAYER IS A BETTER STATE OF MIND

It may be that an individual not in a right state of mind may be benefited by giving himself to prayer. If the prayer is offered with sincerity and solemnity—with a real feeling of want, as it is sometimes in the case of a convicted sinner, it may have a very happy effect upon his own state of mind. When such a man gives himself up to confession and supplication, and spreads out his case before the Lord, it is usually a most important step toward his real conversion. It helps to bring the character and claims of God distinctly before his mind, and has a natural tendency to make his own soul realize more deeply its guilt, its need of pardon, and its duty of submission and of faith in Christ.

But if any person should suppose that a case of this sort is all that is included in prevailing prayer, he mistakes greatly. In prevailing prayer, a child of God comes before Him with real faith in His promises and asks for things agreeable to His will, assured of being heard according to the true intent of the promises.

Thus coming to God, he prevails with Him, and really influences God to do what otherwise He would not do by any means. That is, prayer truly secures from God the bestowing of the blessing sought. Nothing less than this corresponds either with the promises of Scripture or with its recorded facts with respect to the answers made to prevailing prayer.

GOD ANSWERS PRAYER

God is unchangeably in the attitude of answering prayer. This is true for the same reason that He is unchangeably in the attitude of being complacent in holiness whenever He sees it. The reason in both cases lies in His infinitely benevolent nature. For no other reason than He is infinitely good, He is evermore in the attitude of answering suitable prayer, and of being complacent toward all real holiness.

As in the latter case, whenever a moral change takes place in a sinner of such a nature that God can love him, His infinite love gushes forth instantaneously and without bounds. In the former case, as soon as any suppliant places himself in such an attitude that God can wisely answer his prayer, then instantly the ear of

Jehovah inclines to his petition, and the answer is freely given.

To illustrate this point, suppose that for a season some obstacle obstructs the sunbeams from the rosebush at your door; it fades and looks sickly. But take away the obstacle, and instantly the sunbeams fall in their reviving power upon the rose. So sin casts its dark shadow upon the soul, and obstructs the sunbeams of Jehovah's smiles. But take away the obstacle—the sin—and the smiles fall in of course, and in their full blaze on that penitent and morally changed heart. The sun of Jehovah's face shines always — shines in its own nature. And its beams fall on all objects that are not cast into some deep shade by interposing sin and unbelief. On all objects not thus shaded, its glorious beams forever fall in all their sweetness and beauty.

Hence all real prayer moves God, not merely by benefiting the suppliant through its reflex action, but really and in fact inducing Him to grant the blessing sought. The notion that the whole benefit of prayer is its reflex influence upon the suppliant, and not the obtaining of any blessing, is both vain and preposterous. You might as well suppose that all the good you get by removing obstacles that cut off the sunbeams, is the physical exercise attending the effort. You might as well deny that the sunbeams will actually reach every object as soon as you take away that which throws them into the shade.

God does truly hear and answer prayer, even as an earthly parent hears the petition of a dutiful child, and shapes His course to meet the petition. To deny this is to deny the very nature of God. It is equivalent to denying that God is benevolent. Nothing can be more clear than the fact that God promises to be influenced by prayer so as to bestow blessings to the suppliant that are given to none other, and on no other condition. If God is pure and good, then it must follow that—the obstacle of sin being removed in the case of a fallen being—the divine love must flow out toward him as it did not and could not before. God remains forever the same, just as the sun forever shines. His love meets every object that lies open to His beams, just as the sun's rays cheer everything not shaded by positive obstructions.

Again, God may hear the mere cry of distress and speedily send help. He "hears the young ravens when they cry," and the young lions, too, when they roar and seek their meat from God. The storm-tossed mariners, also, "at their wit's end, cry unto the Lord in their trouble, and he bringeth them out of their distress." His benevolence leads Him to do all this, wherever He can without detriment to the interests of His government. Yet this case seems not to come under the promises made to believing prayer. These cases of distress often occur in the experience of wicked men. Yet sometimes God seems obviously to hear their cry. He has wise reasons for doing so; probably often His object is to open their eyes to see their own Father, and to touch their hearts with a sense of their ingratitude in their rebellion against such a God.

No matter what the reason, the fact cannot be disputed. Cases not infrequently occur in which persons not pious are afflicted by the dangerous illnesses of near friends or relatives, and lift their imploring cries of distress to the Lord, and He hears them. It is even said in Scripture that Christ heard the prayer of devils when they "besought him much that he would not send them away out of the country," and said, "send us into the swine, that we may enter into them."

Manifestly, the Lord often hears this kind of prayer, whenever no special reason exists for refusing to hear it. Yet this is far from being that peculiar kind of prayer to which the special promises of hearing and answering prayer are made.

It is however both interesting and instructive to see how often the Lord does hear even such prayer as these cries of distress. When the cattle moan in the fields because there is no water, and because the grass is withered, there is One on high who listens to their moans. Why should He not? Has He not a compassionate heart? Does not His ear bend under the quick impulse of spontaneous affection, when any of His creatures cry unto Him as their Father, and when no great moral considerations forbid His showing favor?

It is striking to see how much the parental character of the great Jehovah is developed in the course of His providence by His hearing this kind of prayer. Great multitudes of facts are exhibited both in the Bible and in history, which set this subject in a strong light. I once knew a wicked man who, under deep affliction from the dangerous illness of his child, set himself to pray that God would spare and restore the dear one; and God appeared to answer His prayer in a most remarkable manner.

Those of you who have read the "Bank of Faith," know that Mr. Huntington, before his conversion, in many instances seemed to experience the same kind of signal answers to his prayers. Another anecdote was told me the past winter which I should relate more freely if it were not somewhat amusing and laughable as well as instructive. A wicked man, who had perhaps not prayed since he was a child, was out with a hunting party on the confines of Iowa, hunting wild buffalo. Mounted on trained horses, lasso in hand, his party came up to a herd of buffalo, and this man encountered a fierce buffalo bull. The animal rushed upon him. Its first push unhorsed him; but quick as thought in his fall, the man seized his own horse's neck, swung under the neck, and there held on in the utmost peril of his life, his horse being at full gallop, pursued by a ferocious wild bull. To break his hold and fall was almost certain death, and he was every moment in the utmost danger of falling under the flying feet of his rushing horse. In this predicament he bethought himself of prayer; but the only words he could think of, were,

"Now I lay me down to sleep,
I pray the Lord my soul to keep"

Perhaps he had never heard much other prayer than this. This lay embalmed among the recollections of his childhood days. Yet even this prayer the Lord in His infinite mercy seemed to hear and answer by rescuing the man unhurt from this perilous condition. The case affords us a striking exemplification not only of the fact that God hears the cry of mere distress, sometimes even when made by wicked men, but also of another fact, namely, that the spirit of a prayer may be a very different thing from its letter. In this case, the letter and the spirit bore no close resemblance. The spirit of the prayer was for deliverance from imminent peril. The Lord seems to have heard.

But it should be continually borne in mind, that these are not the prayers that God has pledged Himself by promise to hear and answer. The latter are evermore the believing prayers of His own children.

THE SPIRIT OF THE PRAYER IS IMPORTANT

Our great inquiry now has respect to this class of prayers, namely, those that God has solemnly promised to answer. Attached to the promises made respecting this class of prayers are certain conditions. These being fulfilled, God holds Himself bound to answer the prayer according to both the letter and spirit, if they both correspond. If they do not correspond, then He will answer according to the spirit of the prayer. This is evermore the meaning of His promise. His promise to answer prayer on certain conditions is a pledge at least to meet it in its true spirit, and do or give what the spirit of the prayer implies.

It now becomes us to inquire most diligently and most earnestly for the conditions of prevailing prayer. This point I shall enter upon in my next discourse.

11

CONDITIONS OF PREVAILING PRAYER

PART 2

From: *The Oberlin Evangelist*
June 9, 1847

> *"Ask, and it shall be given you."*
>
> —Matthew 7:7-8

> *" Ask and receive not, because ye ask amiss, to consume it upon your lusts."*
>
> —James 4:3

I will commence the present discourse by briefly recapitulating the prefatory remarks that I made in my first sermon on this subject. I then observed:

That all real prayer is heard and answered.

1. Prayer is not always answered according to the *letter* of it, but often only according to its *spirit*. As an instance of this, I spoke of the striking case recorded respecting Paul's thorn in the flesh.

2. None can be saved who are not in a state of mind to prevail in prayer.

3. Many things are really answers to prayer that are not recognized by the suppliant as such nor by those who witness the prayer, the blessing bestowed, or the thing done in connection with it.

4. Much that is called prayer is not really prayer at all.

5. Many neither care nor expect to be heard, and therefore do not watch to see whether their prayers are answered. They pray merely as a duty; their heart being set on doing the duty and appeasing their consciences, and not on obtaining the blessing nominally asked for.

6. Nor do such persons feel disappointed if they fail of obtaining what they profess to ask for in prayer.

7. They do not trouble themselves to inquire why they are not answered. If they can only discharge their duty and appease their consciences, they have their desire.

8. Failure to obtain the blessing sought is always because the revealed conditions are not fulfilled.

9. Nothing is more important for us than to attend to, and understand the revealed conditions of prevailing prayer.

10. God may answer the mere cry of distress when benevolence does not forbid it. He often does hear the sailor in the storm—the young ravens in their hunger; but this is a very different thing from

that prayer which God has pledged Himself by promise to hear and answer on the fulfillment of certain conditions.

THE CONDITIONS OF PREVAILING PRAYER

The first condition is a state of mind in which you would offer the Lord's prayer sincerely and acceptably.

Christ at their request taught His disciples how to pray. In doing so, He gave them an epitome of the appropriate subjects of prayer, and also threw a most important light upon the spirit with which all prayer should be offered. This form is exceedingly comprehensive. Every word is full of meaning. It would seem very obvious however that our Lord did not intend here to specify all the particular things we may pray for, but only to group together some of the great heads of subjects which are appropriate to be sought of God in prayer, and also to show us with what temper and spirit we should come before the Lord.

This is evidently not designed as a mere form, to be used always and without variation. It cannot be that Christ intended we should evermore use these words in prayer and no other words; for He never again used these precise words Himself—so far as we know from the sacred record—but did often use other and very different words, as the scriptures abundantly testify.

But this form answers a most admirable purpose if we understand it to be given us to teach us these two most important things, namely, what sort of blessings we may pray for, and in what spirit we should pray for them.

Most surely, then, we cannot hope to pray acceptably unless we can offer this prayer in its real spirit—our own hearts deeply sympathizing with the spirit of this prayer. If we cannot pray the

Lord's prayer sincerely, we cannot offer any acceptable prayer at all.

Hence it becomes us to examine carefully the words of this recorded form of prayer. Yet, be it remembered, it is not these words, as mere words, that God regards, or that we should value. Words themselves, apart from their meaning, and from their meaning as used by us, would neither please nor displease God. He looks on the heart.

THE LORD'S PRAYER

"When ye pray," says our Lord, "use not vain repetitions as the heathen do; for they think that they shall be heard for their much speaking."

Hence there is no need that you continue to clamor unceasingly, "O Baal, hear us; O Baal, hear us." Those were indeed vain repetitions—just such as the heathen use. It is a most singular fact that the Roman Catholic church has fallen into the practice here condemned. Like the priests of Baal, in Elijah's time, they demand and practice everlasting repetitions of the same words, numbering their repetitions of Pater Nosters and Ava Marias by their beads, and estimating the merit of prayer by the quantity and not the quality of their prayers. The more repetitions, the greater the value. This principle, and the practice founded upon it, our Saviour most pointedly condemns.

So, many persons, not Roman Catholics or heathen, seem to lay much more stress upon the amount of prayer than upon its character and quality. They think if there can only be prayer enough, that is, repetitions enough of the same or similar words, the prayer will be certainly effective, and prevalent with God. No mistake can be greater. The entire word of God rebukes this view of the subject in the most pointed manner.

Yet be it well considered, the precept, "Use not vain repetitions," should by no means be construed to discourage the utmost perseverance and fervency of spirit in prayer. The passage does not forbid our renewing our requests from great earnestness of spirit. Our Lord Himself did this in the garden, repeating His supplication "in the same words." Vain repetitions are forbidden, not repetitions that gush from a burdened spirit.

This form of prayer invites us, first of all to address the great God as **"Our Father who art in heaven."** This authorizes us to come as children and address the Most High, feeling that He is a Father to us.

The first petition follows—**"Hallowed be thy name."** What is the exact idea of this language? To hallow is to sanctify, to deem and render sacred.

There is a passage in Peter's Epistle that may throw light on this.

He says, "Sanctify the Lord God in your hearts." The meaning seems plainly to be this—Set apart the Lord God in your hearts as the only true object of supreme, eternal adoration, worship, and praise. Place Him alone on the throne of your hearts. Let Him be the only hallowed object there.

So here in the first petition of the Lord's Prayer, we pray that both all intelligent beings and ourselves may in this sense hallow the name of the Lord God and sanctify Him in their hearts. Our prayer is—Let all adore thee, the infinite Father—as the only object of universal adoration, praise, worship, and love.

OUR FATHER WHO ART IN HEAVEN, HALLOWED BY THY NAME.

This prayer hence implies:

1. A desire that this hallowing of Jehovah's name should be universal.

2. A willingness to concur heartily ourselves in this sentiment. Our own hearts are in deep sympathy with it. Our inmost souls cry out—Let God be honoured, adored, loved, worshipped and revered by all on earth and all in heaven. Of course, praying in this spirit, we shall have the highest reverence for God. Beginning our prayer thus, it will so far be acceptable to God. Without such reverence for Jehovah's name, no prayer can possibly be acceptable. All irreverent praying is mockery, most abhorrent to the pure and exalted Jehovah.

THY KINGDOM COME

What does this language imply?

1. A desire that God's kingdom should be set up in the world, and all men become holy. The will is set upon this as the highest and most to be desired of all objects whatever. It becomes the supreme desire of the soul, and all other things sink into comparative insignificance before it. The mind and the judgment approve and delight in the kingdom of God as in itself infinitely excellent, and then the will harmonizes most perfectly with this decision of intelligence.

Let it be well observed here that our Lord in giving this form of prayer, assumes throughout that we shall use all this language with most profound sincerity. If any man were to use these words and reject their spirit from His heart, His prayer would be an utter abomination before God. Whoever would pray at all, should consider that God looks on the heart, and is a holy God.

2. It is implied in this petition that the suppliant [*Editor's Note: Suppliant is "one who prays."*] does what he can to establish this kingdom. He is actually doing all he can to promote this great end for which he prays. Anything else and he fails entirely of evincing his sincerity. For nothing can be more sure than that every man who prays sincerely for the coming of Jehovah's kingdom, truly desires and wills that it may come; and if so, he will neglect no means in his power to promote and hasten its coming. Hence every man who sincerely offers this petition will lay himself out to promote the object. He will seek by every means to make the truth of God universally prevalent and triumphant.

3. I might also say that the sincere offering of this petition implies a resistance of everything inconsistent with the coming of this kingdom. This you cannot fail to understand.

THY WILL BE DONE IN EARTH AS IT IS IN HEAVEN.

This petition implies that we desire to have God's will done, and that this desire is supreme.

It implies also a delight in having the will of God done by all His creatures, and a corresponding sorrow whenever it fails of being done by any intelligent being.

There is also implied a state of the will in harmony with this desire. A man whose will is averse to having his own desires granted is insincere, even although his desires are real. Such a man is not honest and consistent with himself.

In general I remark respecting this petition that if it is offered sincerely, the following things must be true:

1. The suppliant is willing that God should require all He

does, and as He does. **His heart will acquiesce both in the things required and in the manner in which God requires them.** It would indeed be strange that a man should pray sincerely that God's will might be done, and yet not be willing himself that God should give law, or carry His will into effect. Such inconsistencies never can happen where the heart is truly sincere and honest before God. No, never. The honest hearted suppliant is as willing that God's will should be done as the saints in heaven are. He delights in having it done, more than in all riches—more than in his highest earthly joy.

2. When a man offers this petition sincerely, it is implied that He is really doing, himself, all the known will of God. For if he is acting contrary to his actual knowledge of God's will, it is most certain that he is not sincere in praying that God's will may be done. If he sincerely desires and is willing that God's will should be done, why does he not do it himself?

3. It implies a willingness that God should use His own discretion in the affairs of the universe, and just as really and fully in this world as in heaven itself. You all admit that in heaven God exercises a holy sovereignty. I do not mean an arbitrary unreasonable sovereignty, but I mean a control of all things according to His own infinite wisdom and love—exercising evermore His own discretion, and depending on the counsel of none but Himself. Thus God reigns in heaven.

You also see that in heaven, all created beings exercise the most perfect submission, and confidence in God. They all allow Him to carry out His own plans framed in wisdom and love, and they even rejoice with exceeding joy that He does. It is their highest blessedness.

Such is the state of feeling toward God universally in heaven.

And such it should be on earth. The man who offers this

petition sincerely must approximate very closely to the state of mind that obtains in heaven.

He will rejoice that God appoints all things as He pleases, and that all beings should be, and do, and suffer as God ordains. If man has not such confidence in God as to be willing to control all events with regard to his own family, his friends, and all his interests (in short, for time and eternity), then certainly his heart is not submissive to God. It is hypocrisy for him to pray that God's will may be done on earth as in heaven. It must be hypocrisy in him because his own heart rebels against the sentiment of his own words.

This petition, offered honestly implies nothing less than universal, unqualified submission to God. The heart really submits, and delights in its submission.

No thought is so truly pleasing as that of having God's will done evermore. A sincere offering of this prayer or indeed of any prayer whatever involves the fullest possible submission of all events for time and for eternity to the hands of God.

All real prayer puts God on the throne of the universe, and the suppliant low before Him at His footstool.

4. The offering of this petition sincerely, implies conformity of life to this state of the will. You will readily see that this must be the case, because the will governs the outward life by a law of necessity. The action of this law must be universal so long as man remains a voluntary moral agent. So long therefore the ultimate purpose of the will must control the outward life.

Hence the man who offers this prayer acceptably must live as he prays and according to his own prayers. It would be a strange and most unaccountable thing indeed if the heart should be in a state to offer this prayer sincerely and yet should act itself out in the life directly contrary to its own expressed and supreme preference and purpose.

Such a case is impossible. The very supposition involves the absurdity of assuming that a man's supreme preference shall not control his outward life.

In saying this, however, I do not deny that a man's state of mind may change, so as to differ the next hour from what it is this. He may be in a state one hour to offer this prayer acceptably, and the next hour may act in a manner right over against his prayer.

But if in this latter hour you could know the state of his will, you would find that it is not such that he can pray acceptably— "Thy will be done." No, his will is so changed as to conform to what you see in his outward life.

Hence a man's state of heart may be to some extent known from his external actions. You may at least know that his heart does not sincerely offer this prayer if his life does not conform to the known will of God.

GIVE US THIS DAY OUR DAILY BREAD.

It is plain that this implies dependence on God for all the favors and mercies we either possess or need.

The petition is remarkably comprehensive. It names only bread, and only the bread for "this day," yet none can doubt that it was designed to include also our water and our needful clothing— whatever we really need for our highest health, and usefulness, and enjoyment on earth. For all these we look to God.

Our Saviour doubtless meant to give us in general the subjects of prayer, showing us for what things it is proper for us to pray; and also the spirit with which we should pray. These are plainly the two great points that He aimed chiefly to illustrate in this remarkable form of prayer.

Whoever offers this petition sincerely is in a state of mind to recognize and gratefully acknowledge the providence of God. He sees the hand of God in all the circumstances that affect his earthly state. The rain and the sunshine, the winds and the frosts, he sees coming, all of them, from the hand of his own Father. Hence he looks up in the spirit of a child, saying, **"Give me this day my daily bread."**

But there are those who philosophize and speculate themselves entirely out of this filial dependence on God. They arrive at such ideas of the magnitude of the universe that it becomes in their view too great for God to govern by a minute attention to particular events. Hence they see no God, other than an unknowing Nature in the ordinary processes of vegetation, or in the laws that control animal life. A certain indefinable but unintelligent power which they call Nature does it all. Hence they do not expect God to hear their prayers or notice their wants. Nature will move on in its own determined channel whether they pray or restrain prayer.

Now men who hold such opinions cannot pray the Lord's prayer without the most glaring hypocrisy. How can they offer this prayer and mean anything by it, if they truly believe that everything is nailed down to a fixed chain of events in which no regard is had or can be had to the prayers or wants of man?

Surely, nothing is more plain than that this prayer recognizes most fully the universal providence of that same infinite Father who gives us the promises and who invites us to plead them for obtaining all the blessings we can ever need.

It practically recognizes God as Ruler over all.

What if a man should offer this prayer, but should add to it an appendix of this sort: "Lord, although we ask of thee our daily bread, yet Thou knowest we do not believe Thou hast anything at all to do with giving us each day our daily bread; for we believe Thou art too high and Thy universe too large to admit of our supposing that Thou canst attend to so small a matter as supplying our daily food. We believe that Thou art so unchangeable, and the laws of nature are so fixed that no regard can possibly be had to our prayers or our wants."

Now would this style of prayer correspond with the petitions given us by Christ, or with their obvious spirit?

Plainly this prayer dictated for us by our Lord implies a state of heart that leans upon God for everything—for even the most minute things that can possibly affect our happiness or be to us objects of desire. The mind looks up to the great God, expecting from Him, and from Him alone, every good and perfect gift. For everything we need, our eye turns naturally and spontaneously toward our great Father.

And this is a daily dependence. The state of mind that it implies is habitual.

FORGIVE US OUR DEBTS AS WE FORGIVE OUR DEBTORS.

In this immediate connection, the Saviour says, "For if ye forgive men their trespasses, your Heavenly Father will also forgive you. But if ye forgive not men their trespasses, neither will your Father forgive your trespasses." The word *trespasses*, therefore doubtless explains what is meant by debts in the Lord's prayer.

Luke, in reciting this Lord's prayer, expresses it as, "Forgive us our sins; for we also forgive every one that is indebted to us." These various forms of expression serve to make the meaning quite plain. It may often happen that in such a world as this, some of my fellow men may wrong or at least offend me—in some such way as I wrong and displease God. In such cases this petition of the Lord's prayer implies that I forgive those who injure me, even as I pray to be forgiven myself.

The phraseology in Matthew makes the fact that we forgive others either the measure, or the condition of our being forgiven. In Luke, it seems to be at least a condition if not a ground or reason of the request for personal forgiveness. The former reads, "Forgive us as we forgive," and the latter, "Forgive us, for we also forgive every one indebted to us."

Now on this petition I remark,

1. It cannot possibly imply that God will forgive us our sins while we are still committing them. Suppose one should use this form of petition—"Lord, forgive me for having injured Thee as Thou knowest that I do most freely forgive all men who injure me;" while yet it is perfectly apparent to the man himself and to everybody else that he is still injuring and abusing God as much as ever. Would not such a course be equivalent to saying, "Lord, I am very careful, Thou seest, not to injure my fellow men, and I freely forgive their wrongs against me; but I care not how much I abuse and wrong Thee!" This would be horrible! Yet this horrible prayer is virtually invoked whenever men ask of God forgiveness with the spirit of sin and rebellion in their hearts.

2. This petition never reads thus; "Forgive us our sins and enable us to forgive others also." This would be a most abominable prayer to offer to God. Certainly if it be understood to imply that we cannot forgive others unless we are specially enabled to do so by power given us in answer to prayer; and worse still, if this inability to forgive is imputed to God as its Author.

However the phraseology is explained, and whatever it is understood to imply, it is common enough in the mouths of men, but nowhere found in the book of God.

3. Christ, on the other hand, says, Forgive us as we forgive others. We have often injured, abused, and wronged Thee. Our fellow men have also often injured us, but Thou knowest we have freely forgiven them. Now, therefore, forgive us as Thou seest we have forgiven others. If Thou seest that we do forgive others, then do Thou indeed forgive us and not otherwise. We cannot ask to be ourselves forgiven on any other condition.

4. Many seem to consider themselves quite pious if they can put up with it when they are injured or slighted; if they can possibly control themselves so as not to break out into a passion. If, however, they are really wronged, they imagine they do well to be angry. O, to be sure! Somebody has really wronged them, and shall they not resent it and study how to get revenge, or at least, redress? But notice that the Apostle Peter says, "If when ye do well and suffer for it, ye take it patiently, this is acceptable with God." "For even hereunto were ye called," as if all Christians had received a special call to this holy example. O, how would such an example rebuke the spirit of the world!

5. It is one remarkable condition of being answered in prayer that we suffer ourselves to harbor no ill will to any human being. We must forgive all that wrong us, and forgive them, too, from the heart. God really requires us to love our enemies as to love our friends, really requires us to forgive others as to ask forgiveness for ourselves. Do we always bear this in mind? Are you, beloved, always careful to see to it that your state of mind toward all who may possibly have wronged you is one of real forgiveness, and do you never think of coming to God in prayer until you are sure you have a forgiving spirit yourself?

Plainly, this is one of the ways in which we may test our fitness of heart to prevail with God in prayer. "When thou standest, praying, forgive, if thou hast ought against any." Think not to gain audience before God unless you most fully and heartily forgive all who may be thought to have wronged you.

Sometimes persons of a peculiar temperament hold grudges against others. They have enemies against whom they not only speak evil, but also know not how to speak well. Now, such persons who harbor such grudges in their hearts can no more prevail with God in prayer than the devil can. God would as soon hear the devil pray and answer his prayers rather hear and answer the prayers of those who hold grudges. They need not think to be heard—not they!

How many times have I had occasion to rebuke this unforgiving spirit! Often while in a place, laboring to promote a revival, I have seen the workings of this jealous, unforgiving spirit, and I have felt like saying, Take these things hence! Why do you get up a prayer meeting and think to pray to God when you know that you hate your brother, and know moreover that I know you do? Away with it! Let such professed Christians repent, break down, get into the dust at the feet of God and men before they think to pray acceptably! Until they do thus repent all their prayers are only a "smoke in the nose" before God.

LEAD US NOT INTO TEMPTATION.

And what is implied in this?

A fear and dread of sin—watchfulness against temptation, an anxious solicitude lest by any means we should be overcome and fall into sin. On this point Christ often warned His disciples, and not them only, but what He said unto them, He said unto all: "Watch."

A man unafraid of sin and temptation cannot present this petition in a manner acceptable to God.

You will observe, moreover, that this petition does not by any means imply that God leads men into temptation in order to make them sin, so that we must implore Him not to lead us thus, lest He should do it. No, that is not implied at all; but the spirit of the petition is this: O Lord, *Thou knowest how weak I am, and how prone to sin; therefore let thy providence guard and keep me that I may not indulge in anything whatever that may prove to me a temptation to sin. Deliver us from all iniquity—from all the stratagems of the devil. Throw around us all thy precious guardianship, that we may be kept from sinning against Thee.*

How needful this protection, and how fit that we should pray for it without ceasing!

FOR THINE IS THE KINGDOM, THE POWER, AND THE GLORY FOREVER. AMEN.

Here is an acknowledgment of the universal government of God. The suppliant recognizes His supremacy and rejoices in it.

Thus it is when the mind is in the attitude of prevailing prayer. It is most perfectly natural then for us to regard the character, attributes, and kingdom of God as infinitely sacred and glorious.

How perfectly spontaneous is this feeling in the heart of all whom really pray, "*I ask all this because Thou art a powerful, universal, and holy Sovereign. Thou art the infinite Source of all blessings. Unto Thee, therefore, do I look for all needed good either for myself or my fellow beings!"*

How deeply does the praying heart realize and rejoice in the universal supremacy of the great Jehovah! All power, glory, and dominion are thine, and thine only, for ever and ever, amen and amen. Let my whole soul re-echo, amen. Let the power and the glory be the Lord's alone for evermore. Let my soul forever feel and utter this sentiment with its deepest and most fervent emphasis. Let God reign supreme and adored through all earth and all heaven, henceforth and forever.

REMARKS

1. The state of mind involved in this prayer must be connected with a holy life. Most manifestly it can never co-exist with a sinning life. If you allow yourself in sin, you certainly cannot have access to God in prayer. You cannot enter into the spirit of the Lord's prayer and appropriately utter its petitions.

2. The appropriate offering of this prayer involves a corresponding sensibility—a state of feeling in harmony with it. The mind of the suppliant must sympathize with the spirit of this form of prayer. Otherwise he does, by no means, make this prayer his own.

3. It is nothing better than mockery to use the Lord's prayer as a mere form. So multitudes do use it, especially when public worship is conducted by the use of forms of prayer. Often you may hear this form of prayer repeated over and over in such a way as seems to testify that the mind takes no cognizance of the sentiments that the words should express. The chattering of a parrot could scarcely be more senseless and void of impression on the speaker's mind. How shocking to hear the Lord's prayer chattered over thus! Instead of spreading out before God what they really need, they run over the words of this form, and perhaps of some other set forms, as if the utterance of the right words served to constitute acceptable prayer!

If they had gone into the streets and cursed and sworn by the hour, every man of them would be horribly shocked, and would feel that now assuredly the curse of Jehovah would fall upon them. But in their senseless chattering of this form of prayer by the hour together, they as truly blaspheme God as if they had taken His name in vain in any other way.

Men may mock God in pretending to pray, as truly as in cursing and swearing. God looks on the heart, and He estimates nothing as real prayer into which the heart does not enter. And for many reasons it must be peculiarly provoking to God to have the forms of prayer gone through with no heart of prayer to attend them.

Prayer is a privilege too sacred to be trifled with. The pernicious effects of trifling with prayer are certainly not less than the evils of any other form of profanity. Hence God must abhor all public desecration of this solemn exercise.

Now, brethren, in closing my remarks on this one great condition of prevailing prayer, let me beseech you never to suppose that you pray acceptably unless your heart sympathizes deeply with the sentiments expressed in the Lord's prayer.

Your state of mind must be such that these words will most aptly express it. Your heart must run into the very words, and into all the sentiments of this form of prayer. Our Saviour meant here to teach us how to pray; and here you may come and learn how. Here you may see a map of the things to pray for, and a picture of the spirit in which acceptable prayer is offered.

13

CONDITIONS OF PREVAILING PRAYER

PART 3

From: *The Oberlin Evangelist*
July 21, 1847

> *"Ye ask, and receive not, because ye ask amiss that ye may consume it upon your lusts."*
> —James 4:3

In a former discourse on this text, I mentioned, among other conditions of prevailing prayer, that confession should be made to those whom our sins have injured, and also to God. It is most plain that all sins should be confessed to God, that we may obtain forgiveness and be reconciled to Him; else how can we have communion of soul with Him? And who can for a moment doubt that our confessions should not omit those of our fellow beings whom we have injured?

In the next place I remark that restitution should be made to God and to man.

RESTITUTION

To man we should make restitution in the sense of undoing as far as possible the wrong we have done, and repairing and making good all the evil. If we have impeached character wrongfully, we must recall and undo it. If we have injured another even by mistake, we are bound, if the mistake come to our knowledge, to set it right. Either that or we are criminal in allowing it to remain uncorrected. If the injury done by us to our neighbor affect his property, we must make restitution.

But I wish to call your attention more especially to the restitution that we are to make to God. And in respect to this, I do not mean to imply that we can make good our wrongs against God in the sense of really restoring that which we have withheld or taken away; but we can render to Him whatever yet remains. The time yet to be given us we can devote to Him, although the past has gone beyond recall. Our talents and influence and wealth, yet to be used, we may freely and fully use for God; and manifestly, so much as this, God and reason require of us, and it were vain for us to hope to be accepted in prayer unless we seriously intend to render all the future to God.

Let us look more closely into this subject. How many of you have been robbing God—robbing Him for a long time, and on a large scale? Let us see.

We all belong to God. We are His property in the highest possible sense. He brought us into being, gave us all we have, and made us all we are; so that He is our rightful owner in a far higher sense than that in which any man can own any thing whatever.

All we have and are, therefore, is due to God. If we withhold it, we are just so far forth guilty of robbing God. And all this robbery from God, we are unquestionably bound, as far as possible, to make up.

STEALING FROM GOD

Do any of you still question whether men ever do truly rob God? Examine this point thoroughly. If any of you were to slip into a merchant's store and filch money from his drawer, you could not deny that the act is theft. You take, criminally, from your fellow man what belongs to him and does not at all belong to yourself. Now can it be denied that, whenever by sin you withhold from God what is due to Him, you as really rob God as any one can steal from a merchant's drawer? God owns all men and all their services in a far higher sense than that in which any merchant owns the money in his drawer. God rightfully claims the use of all your talents, wealth, and time for Himself—for His own glory and the good of His creatures. Just so far, therefore, as you use yourselves for yourselves, you as really rob God as if you appropriated to yourself any thing that belongs of right to your neighbor.

Stealing differs from robbery chiefly in this: the former is done secretly—the later by violence, in spite of resistance, or, as the case may be, of remonstrance. If you go secretly, without the knowledge of the owner, and take what is his, you steal; if you take aught of his openly—by force—against his known will, you rob. These two crimes differ not essentially in spirit; either is considered a serious trespass upon the rights of a fellow man. Robbery has usually this aggravation: that it puts the owner in fear. But the case may be such that the owner may do all he wisely can to prevent being robbed, and yet you may rob him without exciting alarm and causing him the additional evil of fear. Even in this case, there might still be the essential ingredient of robbery; forcibly taking from another what is his and not yours.

Now how is it that we sin against God? The true answer is, we tear ourselves away from His service. We wrest our hearts by a species of moral violence away from the claims He lays upon us.

He says, "Ye shall serve me, and no other God but me." This is His first and great command; and verily, none can be greater than this. No claim can be stronger than God's upon us can.

Still, it evermore leaves our will free, so that we can rebel and wrest ourselves away from the service of God, if we will do so. And what is this but real robbery?

Suppose it were possible for me to own a man. I know we all deny the possibility of this, our relations to each other as men being what they are; but for illustration it may be supposed that I have created a man and hence own him in as full a sense as God owns us all. Still he remains a free agent—yet solemnly bound to serve me continually. But despite of my claims on him and of all I can wisely do to retain him in my service, he runs away; tears himself from my service. Is not this real robbery—robbery, too, of a most absolute kind? He owes me everything; he leaves me nothing.

So the sinner robs God. Availing himself of his free agency, he tears himself away from God, despite of all his rightful owner can do to enlist his affections, enforce his own claims, and retain his willing allegiance. This is robbery. It is not done secretly, like stealing, but openly, before the sun; and violently too, as in the case of real robbery. It is done despite of all God can wisely do to prevent it.

Hence all sin is robbery. It can never be any thing less than wresting from God what is rightfully His. It is therefore by no figure of speech that God calls this act robbery. Will a man rob God? "Yet ye have robbed me, even this whole nation." Sin is never any thing less than this—a moral agent owned by the highest possible title, yet tearing himself away from his rightful owner, despite of all persuasions and of all claims.

Hence, if any man would prevail with God, he must bring back himself and all that remains not yet squandered and destroyed. Yes, let him come back saying, "Here I am, Lord; I have played the fool and have erred exceedingly, I am ashamed that I have used up so much of thy time, have consumed in sin so much of that strength of mind and body which is thine; ashamed that I have employed these hands and this tongue and all these members of my body in serving myself and Satan, and have wrested them away from Thy service: Lord, I have done most wickedly and meanly; thou seest that I am ashamed of myself, and I feel that I have wronged Thee beyond expression."

So you should come before God. See that thief, coming back to confess and make restitution. Does he not feel a deep sense of shame and guilt? Now unless you are willing to come back and humbly confess and freely restore to God the full use of all that yet remains, how can you hope to be accepted?

You may well be thankful that God does not require of you that you restore all you have wrested from Him and guiltily squandered; all your wasted time and health perhaps, and influence—if He were to demand this, it would at once render your acceptance before Him, and your salvation too, impossible. It would be forever impossible, on such a condition, that you should prevail in prayer.

Blessed be God, He does not demand this. He is willing to forgive all the past—but remember, only on the condition that you bring back all the rest—all that yet remains to be used of yourself and of the powers God has given or may yet give you.

So much as this God must require as a condition; and why should He not? Suppose you have robbed a man of all you can possibly get away from him; and you know that he knows all the facts. Yet you come before him without a confession or a blush and ask him to receive you to his confidence and friendship. He turns upon you—Are not you the man who robbed me? You come to me as if you have never wronged me, and as if you had done nothing to forfeit my confidence and favor; do you come and ask my friendship again? Monstrous!

GOD CAN FORGIVE TRESPASSES

Now would it be strange if God were, in a similar case, to repel an unhumbled sinner in the same way? Can the sinner who comes back to God with no heart to make any restitution, or any consecration of himself to God, expect to be accepted? Nothing can be more unreasonable.

It is indeed nothing less than infinite goodness that God can forgive trespasses so great, so enormous as ours have been—O what a spectacle of loving-kindness is this! Suppose a man had stolen from you ten thousand pounds, and having squandered it all, should be thrown in his rags and beggary at your door. There you see him wasted and wan, hungry and filthy, penniless and wretched; and your heart is touched with compassion. You freely forgive all. You take him up; you weep over his miseries; you wash him, clothe him, and make him welcome to your house and to all the comforts you can bestow upon him. How would all the world admire your conduct as generous and noble in the very highest degree!

But O, the loving-kindness of God in welcoming to His bosom the penitent, returning sinner! How it must look in the eyes of angels! They see the prodigal returning, and hear him welcomed openly to the bosom of Jehovah's family. They see him coming along, wan, haggard, guilty, ashamed, in tattered and filthy robes, and downcast mien—nothing attractive in his appearance; he does not look as if he ever was a son, so terribly has sin defaced the lineaments of sonship; but he comes, and they witness the scene that follows. The Father spies him from afar, and rushes forth to meet him. He owns him as a son; falls upon his neck, pours out tears of gladness at his return, orders the best robe and the fatted calf, and fills his mansion with all the testimonies of rejoicing.

Angels see this—and O, with what emotions of wonder and delight! What a spectacle must this be to the whole universe—to see God coming forth thus to meet the returning penitent! To see that He not only comes forth to take notice of him, but to answer his requests and enter into such communion with him, and such relations, that this once apostate sinner may now ask what he will and it shall be done unto him.

I have sometimes thought that if I had been present when Joseph made himself known to his brethren, I should have been utterly overwhelmed. I can never read the account of that scene without weeping.

I might say the same of the story of the prodigal son. Who can read it without tears of sympathy? O, to have seen it with one's own eyes—to have been there, to have seen the son approaching, pale and trembling; the father rushing forth to meet him with such irrepressible tenderness and compassion; such a spectacle would be too much to endure!

And now let me ask—What if the intelligent universe might see the great God receiving to His bosom a returning, penitent sinner. O, what an interest must such a scene create throughout all heaven! But just such scenes are transpiring in heaven continually. We are definitely told there is joy in the presence of the angels of God over one sinner that repents. Surely all heaven must be one perpetual glow of excitement—such manifestations are ever going forward there of infinite compassion toward sinners returning from their evil ways.

Yet be it evermore remembered, no sinner can find a welcome

before the face of God unless he returns most deeply penitent. Ah! You do not know God at all if you suppose He can receive you without the most thorough penitence and the most ample restitution. You must bring back all that remains unwasted and unsquandered. You must look it all over most carefully and honestly, and say—Here, Lord, is the pitiful remnant—the small amount left: all the rest I have basely and most unprofitably wasted and used up in my course of sin and rebellion. Thou seest how much I have squandered, and how very little is left to be devoted now to thy service. O! What an unprofitable servant I have been; and how miserably unprofitable have I made myself for all the rest of my life.

COMMITTING YOUR FUTURE TO GOD

It were well for every hearer to go minutely into this subject. Estimate and see how many years of your life have gone, never to be recalled. Some of these young people have more years remaining, according to the common laws of life, than we who are farther advanced in years. Yet even you have sad occasion to say—Alas, how many of the best years of my life are thrown away, yes, worse than thrown into the sea; for in fact they have been given to the service of the devil. How many suits of clothing worn out in the ways of sin and the work of Satan. How many tons of provisions—food for man, provided under the bounty of a gracious Providence—have I used up in my career of rebellion against my Maker and Father! O, if it were all now to rise up before me and enter with me into judgment—if each day's daily bread, used up in sin, were to appear in testimony against me; what a scene must the solemn reckoning be!

Let each sinner look this ground all over, and think of the position he must occupy before an abused yet most gracious God, and then say—How can you expect to prevail with God if you do not bring back with a most penitent and devoted heart, all that remains yet to you of years and of strength for God.

How much more, if more be possible, is this true of those who are advanced in years? How fearfully have we wasted our substance and our days in vain! How then shall we hope to conciliate the favor of God and prevail with Him in prayer, unless we bring back all that remains to us, and consecrate it a whole offering to the Lord our God?

We must pass now to another condition of prevailing prayer; namely, that we be reconciled to our brother.

On this subject you will at once recollect the explicit instructions of our Lord; "If thou bring thy gift to the altar, and there rememberest that they brother hath aught against thee; leave there thy gift before the alter, and go thy way; first be reconciled to thy brother, and then come and offer thy gift."

This passage states very distinctly one important condition of acceptable prayer, and shows that all men are not at all times in a fit state to pray. They may be in a state in which they have no right to pray at all. If they were to come before the Lord's altar in this state, He would bid them suspend their offering of prayer, go back at once, and be reconciled to their brother.

THE RIGHT TO PRAY

It is important for men to understand that they should approach God in prayer only when they have a right to pray. Others seem entirely to misconceive the relations of prayer to God and to themselves, and think that their prayers are a great favor to God. They seem to suppose that they lay the Lord under great obligations to themselves by their prayers, and if they have made many prayers, and long, they think it quite hard if the Lord does not acknowledge His obligation to them, and grant them a speedy answer. Indeed, they seem almost ready to fall into a quarrel with God if He does not answer their prayers.

I knew one man who on one occasion prayed all night. Morning came, but no answer from God. For this he was so angry with God, that he was tempted to cut his own throat. Indeed, so excited were his feelings and so sharp was this temptation, that he threw away his knife the better to resist it. This shows how absurdly men feel and think on this subject.

Suppose you owed a man a thousand dollars, and should take it into your head to discharge the debt by begging him to release and forgive it. You renew your prayer every time you see him, and if he is at any distance you send him a begging letter by every mail. Now inasmuch as you have done your part as you suppose, you fall into a passion if he won't do his and freely relinquish your debt. Would not this be on your part sufficiently absurd, sufficiently ridiculous and wrong?

So with the sinner and God. Many seem to suppose that God ought to forgive. They will have it that He is under obligation to them to pardon and put away from His sight all their sins the moment they choose to say.

Now God has indeed promised on certain conditions to forgive; and the conditions being fulfilled, He certainly will fulfill His promise; yet never because it is claimed as a matter of justice or right. His promises all pertain to an economy of mercy and not of strict justice.

When men pray aright, God will hear and answer; but if they pray as a mere duty, or pray to make it a demand on the score of justice, they fundamentally mistake the very idea of prayer.

But I must return to the point under consideration.

Sometimes we have no right to pray. "When thou bringest thy gift to the altar, and there rememberest that thy brother hath aught against thee, leave there thy gift, and go, first be reconciled to thy brother, and then come and offer thy gift." The meaning of this precept seems to be plain. If you are conscious of having wronged your brother, go at once and undo that wrong. If you know that he has any good reason for having aught against you, go and remove that reason as far as lies in your power to do so. Else how can you come before God to ask favors of Him?

Here it is important to understand certain cases that though they may seem, yet do not really come under the spirit of this rule. Another man may suppose himself to have been injured by me, yet I may be entirely conscientious in feeling that I have done no otherwise than right toward him, and still I may be utterly unable to remove from his mind the impression that I have wronged him. In this case, I am by no means cut off from the privilege of prayer.

Thus it often happens when I preach against backsliders that they feel exceedingly hurt and think I have wronged them unpardonably; whereas I may have been only honest and faithful to my Master and to their own souls. In such a case I am not to be debarred the privileges of prayer in consequence of their feelings toward me. It is indeed most absurd that this should shut me away from the mercy-seat. If I am conscious of having done no wrong, the Lord will draw me near to Himself. In such a case as this I can make no confession of wrong-doing.

But the case contemplated by our Lord is one in which I know I have done wrong to my neighbor. Knowing this, I have no right to come before God to pray until I have made restitution and satisfaction.

Sometimes professors of religion have come to me and asked, "Why are we not heard and answered? We pray a great deal, yet the Lord does not answer our prayers."

Indeed, I have asked them, "Do you not recollect many times when in the act of prayer you have been reminded of having injured a brother, and yet you did not go to him and make restitution, or even confession?"

"Yes," Many have said. "I can recollect such cases; but I passed them over, and did not trouble myself with them, I do not know that I thought much about the necessity of making confession and restitution, at all events I know I soon forgot those thoughts of having wronged my neighbor."

CONFESSION AND RESTITUTION

You did, indeed; but God did not forget. He remembered your dishonesty and your neglect, or perhaps contempt of one of His plainly taught conditions of acceptable prayer, and He could not hear you. Until you had gone and become reconciled to your brother, what have you to do with praying? Your God says to you, "Why do you come here before me to lie to my very face, pretending to be honest and upright toward your fellow-beings, when you know you have wronged them, and have never made confession and restitution?"

In my labors as an Evangelist, I have sometimes fallen into a community who were most of them in this horrible state. Perhaps they had sent for me to come among them saying that they were all ready and ripe for a revival, and thus constrained me to go. On coming among them I have found the very opposite to be the fact. I would preach to the impenitent; many would be convicted; and awful solemnity would prevail; but no conversions. Then I would turn to the church and beg them to pray, and soon the fact would come out that they had no fellowship with each other and no mutual confidence; almost every brother and sister had hard feelings toward each other; many knew they had wronged their brethren and had never made confession or restitution; some had not even spoken kindly to one another for months; in short it was a state of real war; and how could the Dove of Peace abide there? And how could a righteous God hear their prayers? He could do no such thing till they repented in dust and ashes, and put away these abominable iniquities from before His face.

It often happens that professors of religion are exceedingly careless in respect to the conditions of prevailing prayer. What! Christian men and women in such a state that they will not speak to each other! In such relations to each other that they are ready to injure one another in the worst way—ready to mangle and rend each other's characters! Away with it! It is an offence to God! It is an utter abomination in His sight! He loathes the prayers and the professed worship of such men, as He loathes idolatry itself.

Now although cases as outrageous as those I have described do not occur frequently, yet many cases do occur which involve substantially the same principle. In respect to all such, let it be known that God is infinitely honest, and so long as He is so, He will not hold communion and fellowship with one who is dishonest.

He expects us to be honest and truthful, willing ever to obey Him, and ever anxious to meet all the conditions of acceptable prayer. Until this is the case with us, He cannot and will not hear us, however much and long we pray. Why should He? "Thou requirest truth in the inward parts," said the Psalmist of his God, as if fully aware that entire sincerity of heart, and of course uprightness of life toward others, is an unalterable condition of acceptance before God

It is amazing to see how much insincerity there often is among professed Christians, both in their mutual relations to each other, and also in the relations to God.

Again, we ought always to have an honest and good reason for praying and for asking for the specific things we pray for. It should be remembered that God is infinitely reasonable, and therefore does nothing without a reason. Therefore in all prayer you should always have a reason or reasons that will commend themselves to God as a valid ground for His hearing and answering your prayers.

COMMENDING REASONS AND GROUNDS FOR PRAYER

You can have a rational confidence that God will hear you only when you know what your reasons are for praying and have good grounds to suppose they are such as will commend themselves to an infinitely wise and righteous God.

Beloved, are you in the habit of giving your attention sufficiently to this point? When you pray, do you ask for your own reasons? Do you inquire: Now have I such reasons for this prayer as God can sympathize with—such as I can suppose will have weight with His mind?

Surely this is an all-important inquiry. God will not hear us unless He sees that we have such reasons as will satisfy His own infinite intelligence—such reasons that He can wisely act in view of them, such that He will not be ashamed to have the universe know that on such grounds He answered our prayers. They must be such that He will not be ashamed of them Himself. For we should evermore consider that all God's doings are one day to be perfectly known. It will yet be known why He answered every acceptable prayer, and why He refused to answer each one that was not acceptable.

Hence if we are to offer prayer, or to do any thing else in which we expect God to sympathize with us, we ought to have good and sufficient reasons for what we ask or do.

You can not help seeing this at your first glance at the subject. Your prayer must not be selfish but benevolent—else how can God hear it? Will He lend himself to patronize and befriend your selfishness?

Suppose a man asks for the Holy Spirit to guide him in any work; or suppose he ask for that Spirit to sanctify himself or his friends. Let him be always able to give a good reason for what he asks. Is his ultimate reason a selfish one—for example, that he may become more distinguished in the world, or may prosecute some favorite scheme for himself and his own glory or his own selfish good? Let him know that the Lord has no sympathy with such reasons for prayer.

Thus a child comes before its parent, and says, "Do give me this or that favor."

"Your reason, my child," says the parent. "Give me your reason; what do you want it for?"

So God says to us, His children, "Your reason, my child; what is your reason?"

You ask. It may be for an education. Why do you want an education? You say, "Lord furnish me the means to pay my tuition bills and by board bills and my clothing bills, for I want to get an education."

"Your reason, my child," the Lord will answer. "Your reason; for what end to you want to get an education?"

You must be able to give a good reason. If you want these things you ask for, only that you may consume them upon your lusts; if your object be to climb up to some higher post among men, or to get your living with less toil, or with more respectability, small ground have you to expect that the Lord will sympathize with any such reasons. But if your reasons are good: if they are such that God will not be ashamed to recognize them as His own reasons for acting, then you will find Him infinitely ready to hear and to answer. O, He will bow His ear with infinite grace and compassion.

Your hope of success in prayer therefore should not lie in the amount, but in the quality of your prayers. If you have been in the habit of praying without regard to the reasons that you ask, you have probably been in the habit of mocking God. Unless you have an errand when you come before the Lord, it is mocking to come and ask for anything. There should always be something that you need. Now, therefore, ask yourself, "Why do I want this thing which I ask of God? Do I need it? For what end do I need it?"

A woman of my acquaintance was praying for the conversion of an impenitent husband. She said, "It would be so much more pleasant for me to have him go to meeting with me, and to have him think and feel as I do." When she was asked, "Is your heart broken because your husband abuses God, because he dishonours Jesus Christ," she replied that she never had thought of that— never; her husband had troubled and grieved her, she knew; but she had not once thought of his having abused and provoked the great and holy God.

How infinitely different must that woman's state of mind become before the Lord can hear and answer her prayer! Can she expect an answer so long as she takes only a selfish view of the case? No, never until she can say, "O my God, my heart is full of bleeding and grief because my husband dishonours Thee; my soul is in agony because he scorns the dying blood and the perfect sacrifice of Jesus Christ."

IN SYMPATHY WITH GOD

So when parents urge their requests for the salvation of their children, let them know that if they sympathize with God, He will sympathize with them. If they are chiefly distressed because their children do not love and serve their own God and Saviour, the Lord will most assuredly enter into the deep sympathies of their hearts, and will delight to answer their requests. So of the wife when she prays for her husband, so universally when friend prays for friend.

The great God seems to say evermore—"If you sympathize with me, I sympathize with you." He is a being of infinite sympathies, and never can fail to reciprocate the holy feelings of His creatures. Let the humblest subject in His universe feel sincere regard for the honour and glory of God and the well being of His kingdom, and how suddenly is it reciprocated by the Infinite Father of all! Let one of all the myriad of His creatures in earth or heaven be zealous for God, then assuredly will God be zealous for him, and will find means to fulfill His promise—"Those who honour me I will honour." But if you will not feel for Him and will not take His part, it is vain for you to ask or expect that He will feel for you and take your part.

It is indeed a blessed consideration that when we go out of ourselves and merge our interest in the interests of God and of His kingdom, then He gathers Himself all round about us, throws His banner of love over us, and draws our hearts into inexpressible nearness of communion with Himself. Then the Eternal God becomes our own God, and underneath us are His almighty arms. Then whoever should "touch us, would touch the apple of His eye." There can be no love more watchful, strong, or tender than that borne by the God of infinite love toward His affectionate, trustful children. He would move heaven and earth if need be, to hear prayer offered in such a spirit.

O for a heart to immerse and bathe ourselves, as it were, in the sympathies of Jehovah—to yield up really our whole hearts to Him, until our deepest and most perfect emotions should gush and flow out only in perfect harmony with His will, and we should be swallowed up in God, knowing no will but His, and no feelings but in sympathy with His. Then wave after wave of blessings would roll over us, and God would delight to let the universe see how intensely He is pleased with such a spirit in His creatures.

O then you would need only put yourself in an attitude to be blessed and you could not fail of receiving all you could ask that could be really a good to your soul and to God's kingdom. Almost before you should call, He would answer and while you were yet speaking He would hear. Opening wide your soul in large expectation and strong faith before God, you might take a large blessing, even "until there should not be room enough to receive it.

Study Guide

The following questions are designed to help you reflect upon Finney's sermons on revival through prayer. Some questions are factual in nature; others require some interpretation and application of the material. All the questions will aid you in understanding the teachings of this great man.

Introduction

1. What were some of the influences that led Finney to become interested in the study of the Scriptures?

2. As Finney began the study of elementary law, what important discovery did he make?

3. Describe Finney's personal experience of being baptized in the Holy Spirit.

4. In 1830 Finney experienced the apex of his ministry. Describe what happened as a result of the Rochester revival.

Chapter 1
The Communicable Secret of Mr. Finney's Power

1. What is the ultimate source of all power?

2. What are the four words beginning with the letter C that marked Finney's life and ministry?

3. What are the four words beginning with the letter S that helped to provide Finney with the power to be a great preacher?

4. What was the main maxim that motivated Finney's ministry?

Chapter 2
Delighting in the Lord

1. What is the promise of God that Finney discusses in this chapter?

2. What nine implications are involved in delighting ourselves in the Lord?

3. What condition is necessary before we can receive the desires of our heart?

4. What is one's supreme desire when he or she takes delight in God?

5. What are some of the direct results that come from delighting oneself in God?

Chapter 3
The Joy of God's Salvation

1. Why did the Psalmist pray to have his joy restored?

2. What are the six principal ingredients or elements that enter into the joy of God's salvation?

3. There are five conditions that must be met before the prayer to have one's joy restored can be answered. What are they?

4. Is it selfish to desire to have one's joy restored? Why?

Chapter 4
The Reward of Fervent Prayer

1. What is implied in the command, "Open thy mouth wide"?

2. In what sense is God honored by big requests?

3. Why is God dishonored by feeble requests?

4. What would happen if all Christians were to avail themselves of all the blessings which God has provided and become filled with the Holy Spirit?

Chapter 5
The Prayer of Faith

1. What should we believe when we pray?

2. Why is faith an indispensable condition of effective prayer?

3. How do we develop a state of mind that enables us to exercise real faith?

4. What is the difference between faith and presumption?

Chapter 6
The Spirit of Prayer

1. What does the Holy Spirit do in behalf of the saints?

2. How does the Holy Spirit help us in our infirmities?

3. How do we obtain the help of the Holy Spirit in our prayers?

4. For whom does the Holy Spirit intercede?

5. In praying for something, is it necessary to persevere until it is obtained?

6. What are the three classes of people in the Church who are liable to error with regard to the subject of the Spirit of prayer?

Chapter 7
An Approving Heart—Confidence in Prayer

1. When we have confidence that our heart does not condemn us, what other kind of confidence do we have?

2. When does God hear our prayers?

3. Why does God always answer the kind of prayer that is described in 1 John 3:21-22?

4. Why should we pray in Jesus' name?

Chapter 8
On Prayer

1. Why did Jesus command us to pray so much and so often?

2. What specific benefits are derived from prayer?

3. Why do people sometimes avoid prayer?

Chapter 9
Prevailing Prayer

1. What two goals are prerequisites to revival?

2. What is meant by "prevailing prayer"?

3. What are the essential attributes of prevailing prayer?

4. What is persevering prayer?

5. What are some of the reasons why God requires us to engage in prevailing prayer?

Chapter 10
Conditions of Prevailing Prayer (Part 1)

1. What conditions are required in prevailing prayer?

2. What is the difference between the letter and the spirit of prayer?

3. How do we know that God answers prayer?

Chapter 11
Conditions of Prevailing Prayer (Part 2)

1. Why is the Lord's Prayer a good model prayer for Christians?

2. What is the meaning of this phrase, "Thy kingdom come"?

3. What must one completely forsake in order to enter into the spirit of the Lord's Prayer?

4. Why should the Lord's Prayer never be used as a mere form?

Chapter 12
Conditions of Prevailing Prayer (Part 3)

1. Why is making restitution an important part of the life of prayer?

2. In what ways do people steal from God?

3. What is the role of confession?

4. What does Finney mean when he says we should be "in sympathy with God"?

INDEX

Q

R

T

U

Pure Gold Classics

AN
EXPANDING
COLLECTION
OF THE
BEST-LOVED
CHRISTIAN
CLASSICS OF
ALL TIME.

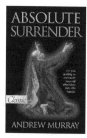

ABSOLUTE SURRENDER
Classic
ANDREW MURRAY

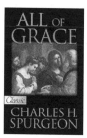

ALL OF GRACE
Classic
CHARLES H. SPURGEON

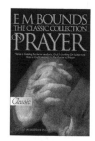

E M BOUNDS THE CLASSIC COLLECTION ON PRAYER
Classic

JOHN CALVIN GOD THE CREATOR GOD THE REDEEMER
Classic
INSTITUTES OF THE CHRISTIAN RELIGION

THE CHRISTIAN'S SECRET OF A HAPPY LIFE
Classic
HANNAH WHITALL SMITH

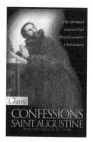

CONFESSIONS SAINT AUGUSTINE
The Spiritual journey that shaped western Christianity
Classic

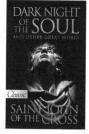

DARK NIGHT OF THE SOUL AND OTHER GREAT WORKS
Classic
SAINT JOHN OF THE CROSS

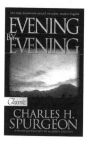

EVENING BY EVENING
Classic
CHARLES H. SPURGEON

SPIRITUAL LETTERS CHRISTIAN COUNSEL MAXIMS OF THE SAINTS
Classic
THE BEST OF FENELON
FRANCOIS DE SALIGNAC DE LA MOTHE-FENELON

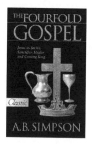

THE FOURFOLD GOSPEL
Jesus as Savior, Sanctifier, Healer and Coming King
Classic
A.B. SIMPSON

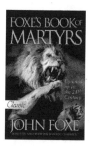

FOXE'S BOOK OF MARTYRS
Classic
JOHN FOXE

GOD OF ALL COMFORT
Classic
HANNAH WHITALL SMITH

THE GREATEST THING IN THE WORLD
Classic
HENRY DRUMMOND

THE HOLY SPIRIT POWER
10 additional Timeless Messages
Prologue by Charles Wesley
Classic
JOHN WESLEY

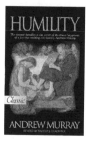

HUMILITY
Classic
ANDREW MURRAY

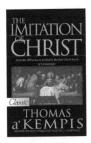
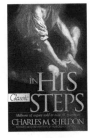
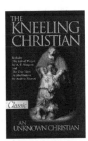

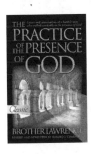

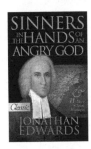

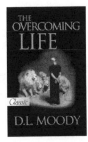

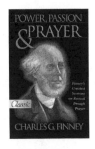
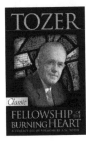
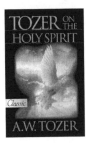
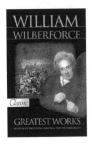
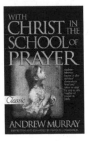